THE ILLUSTRATED BOOK OF Preserves

Preserving food is an age-old practice which, despite the advent of freezers, is still of the greatest interest to all who truly care about good food. For not only does preserving make use of fruit and vegetables in season, when they are plentiful and cheap; it also allows the individual to experiment – with mixtures, with colours, with flavours. And of course whatever we choose to preserve ourselves will be entirely free of the artificial preservatives and colouring agents which plague so much of what we eat today.

This book tells, simply and clearly and with the help of numerous colour photographs and illustrations, how to take advantage of the seasons and enjoy the satisfaction of bottling one's own fruit and vegetables.

Simonetta Lupi was editor of *Cucina Italiana*, Italy's foremost cookery magazine, before becoming editor-in-chief on cookery for the Italian publisher Fabbri. Author and editor of many books on food, she also acts as a food consultant for many major Italian companies.

Angelo Sorzio began his culinary career peeling potatoes as a kitchen boy; today he is head chef at the Grand Hotel des Bains on the Lido in Venice, a position which places him at the top of his profession.

THE ILLUSTRATED BOOK OF Preserves

SIMONETTA LUPI • ANGELO SORZIO

AURUM PRESS

Contents

Introduction 5

Preserving fruit 7

Preserves and jams made with orchard and exotic fruits 13

Jams and preserves made with wild fruits 33

Preserves and jams made with garden fruits and flowers 41

Preserves and jams made with vegetables 47

Jellies made with wild and garden produce 53

Fruit preserved in syrup 63

Fruit preserved in spirits and liqueurs 77

Candied and dried fruit 97

Unusual preserves 105

Preserving vegetables 115

Preserving vegetables in salt, cooking liquid or brine 121

Vegetables preserved in oil 139

Pickled and marinated vegetables 149

Dried vegetables and flavoured vinegars 161

Gourmet preserved foods 167

How it's done – step by step 185

Orange and lemon marmalade 186

Citron marmalade 187

Green tomato jam 188

Oranges preserved in alcohol 189

Grapes in grappa 190

Dried apples 191

Artichokes in light brine 192

Cauliflower in oil 194

Button mushrooms in vinegar 195

Sweet-sour onions 196

Puglia sweet (bell) peppers 197

Botanical guide 198

Index 206

Note on weights and measures: Measurements are given in American, Imperial and metric versions. It is important to follow one version only as the quantities are not interchangeable.

Translated by Sara Harris
Published in 1986 by Aurum Press Limited, 33 Museum Street, London WC1A 1LD

Photographs by Piero Baguzzi, Alberto Bertoldi, Roberto Esposito, Mario Matteucci and Romano Vada

ISBN 0-948149 32 9

Production Services by Studio Asterisco, Milan

Printed in Italy by Gruppo Editoriale Fabbri S.p.A., Milan

Is home preserving necessary any longer? Is it just a hobby nowadays? With thousands of different products marketed by the food industry, do we really need to revive all those age-old preserving recipes handed down over the generations? Obviously the answer depends on your lifestyle, but one of the best reasons for making our own preserves is that we know exactly what's in them: carefully prepared, unadulterated ingredients. This implies no criticism of the food processing companies, who have to follow set procedures to guarantee consistently reliable products; there is no doubt, however, that the art of home preserving still flourishes, perpetuating the expertise of our grandmothers and great-grandmothers, back through countless generations. Admittedly, it is sometimes difficult to find time for home preserving, which is a pity as this is a relaxing, enjoyable and useful pastime. When confronted by row upon row of jars on supermarket shelves, we are often at a loss which to choose. Apricot or peach jam? Lemon or orange marmalade? They all seem to taste rather similar and tend to be oversweetened.

So why not go back to the old, homely tradition and rediscover at long last the elusive and delicate aroma of wild fruit; the penetrating flavour of quinces; the authentic savour of vegetables; the tang of citron; the velvety taste of peaches and apricots and the exciting aroma of exotic fruits. Once started, you will find it needs no special talent, nor even a great deal of time or trouble; just a little patience, care and, perhaps, a dash of imagination to add a special touch to your own preserves.

Vegetables and fruit can be preserved with sugar; sugar and alcohol; sugar and liqueurs; with oil, wine vinegar or salt; by sun-drying and, for more risky raw materials, by sterilization. This book will help you to rediscover the tastes, colours and aromas of each season's fruits and vegetables. You can experiment with unusual combinations, new methods and different techniques, and have the satisfaction of tasting and serving pure, wholesome, natural food prepared with care and discernment.

Preserving fruit

Making jams and jellies and preserving fruit in alcohol

There are many ways of preserving fruit, some of them more widely practised than others nowadays. They can be preserved whole and uncooked in a sugar syrup or alcohol; candied, crystallized or dried; or turned into jams, marmalades, jellies, conserves, sauces and purées. Each method has its own set of rules which applies regardless of the type of fruit being processed, and which ensures safety and success.

Above all, never forget that fruit is very perishable because of its chemical composition: it is 80-90 per cent water, which enables bacteria and enzymes to start breaking down the fruit and leads to deterioration in its texture and taste.

Ideally the fruit should be picked just before processing, from your own garden or a nearby fruit farm, to ensure that it has not been handled a lot or, worse still, spent a long time in transit with the result that it is no longer really fresh.

Never use forced or greenhouse-grown early fruits, which are not only very expensive but also have much less taste.

Selecting and gathering the fruit

The best time to pick fruit is in the early morning, as soon as the dew has been dried by the sun. Choose the best fruit, ripe but not overripe (unless the recipe states otherwise); it must be sound, free from fungicides and other chemicals. Gather your fruit at the height ot its season. Be sure to check that citrus fruits have not been treated with diphenyl.

Adjust your picking methods to suit the preserving method you have chosen: the fruit can, of course, be gathered without leaving the stem attached for jams, jellies and conserves, but when preserving in syrup or alcohol (be it brandy, marc or vodka, etc.) the fruit should be left on the

stem, which is then trimmed to within a fraction of the fruit with small sharp scissors.

First steps

So long as you are dealing with untreated fruit from your own garden, avoid washing it if possible or, where feasible, wipe it with a damp cloth. If the fruit has to be washed, rinse it thoroughly but very briefly to avoid damaging the fruit or impairing the flavour. For most jams, conserves and marmalades and all jellies, you will need to remove pits or stones, seeds, pips and stalks; the fruit does not always have to be peeled. Chopping or slicing is the next step, with the obvious exceptions of strawberries, cherries and other very small fruits. When preserving in syrup or alcohol, leave the fruit whole unless the recipe states otherwise.

Equipment for preparing and preserving fruit

Make sure you have:

- two very sharp stainless steel knives (blades measuring 6in / 15cm and 4in / 10cm), one with a serrated edge
- a potato peeler (for peeling citrus fruit)
- an apple corer
- two long-handled wooden spoons
- a large, long-handled wooden spatula for stirring
- a stainless steel ladle for transferring the jam into jars
- a copper preserving kettle or pan (or a very large, wide, stainless steel kettle or pan) which should have a flat, hollow-ground base (both these provide a wide surface area for evaporation of moisture when the fruit is cooked)
- two large stainless steel saucepans for blanching and boiling whole fruit
- three hair sieves, of varying fine gauges, to purée the fruit (sometimes a food mill will do instead)
- a large, stainless steel fine-mesh sieve for draining
- a skimmer or fine-mesh shallow ladle or slotted/perforated spoon for removing the fruit from its poaching syrup and removing foam or scum
- a calico, canvas or flannel jelly bag for straining jellies
- a colander for draining fruit after washing or blanching when the fruit is to be preserved without further cooking
- a measuring jug or bowl for accurate calculation of liquids
- a stainless steel grater for grating the flesh of certain fruits and the rind of citrus fruits
- a large hardwood chopping block
- a syrup gauge or sucrometer to measure the density of sugar syrup: when lowered into the syrup, it becomes submerged to varying depths, depending on the density of the liquid; you can then gauge the density by the reading on the level scale

- two or three glass, Pyrex or china bowls
- scales or measuring cups and spoons
- a small bottle-corking machine (or patent bottle sealers)
- two or three cloths, preferably calico or flannel
- a sterilizer or a large, flat-bottomed kettle/pan
- a candy or sugar thermometer
- assorted sizes of jars, bottles etc.
- paper filters, or fine cheesecloth/muslin/calico for syrup and juice preparation

A few hints

- Wash the fruit before removing stalks or hulling, etc. Always scrub citrus fruit under running water to get rid of all traces of fungicidal sprays from the pores of the rind.
- Tie cores and seeds or pips in a cheesecloth/muslin bag and cook with the fruit, removing, squeezing and then discarding when the jam or marmalade has reached setting point; the pectin they contain greatly improves the set.
- Where possible, use patent preserving jars which are designed to withstand high temperatures. Choose wide-necked types with the special rubber-rimmed lids and screw collars (or with rubber rings, glass lid and clamps) in ½ pint / ¼ litre or 1 pint / ½ litre sizes. Store the rubber rings or rubber-rimmed lids in their plastic containers in a dry place. Stack the rubber rings; don't hang them on hooks as this pulls them out of shape. Never use metal lids with bonded rubber surrounds twice.
- Before using the jars, wash in cold water, then immerse for a few minutes in lukewarm water containing a little baking soda / bicarbonate of soda; rinse in cold water again.
- When cooking the fruit, use equipment and utensils which will not react with the acid in the fruit: copper (although fruits high in Vitamin C may lose some of their vitamin content when cooked in copper), stainless steel or earthenware. Rinse copper kettles/preserving pans with plenty of water mixed with vinegar before use.
- Never have the preserving pan more than, say, two-thirds full; the mixture often bubbles up and could overflow.
- When filling each jar with hot jam, stand a stainless spoon in it; this will act as a heat conductor and help prevent cracking.
- If using a copper kettle or pan, never leave the jam or jelly to stand in it once it has reached setting point and finished cooking; transfer the contents to a large china, earthenware or Pyrex bowl.
- Never fill jars to the brim. Before sealing, wipe off any drips inside and out before they have a chance to set and harden, using a clean cloth dampened with boiling water.
- Label each jar with a "use by" date and the date made.

Citron marmalade

Jams and other fruit preserves

First of all, there is a difference between jams and preserves, although the names are often used indiscriminately. For jam, the fruit is usually crushed or chopped and always cooked for long enough with sugar to result in a fairly homogeneous consistency which will spread easily, sometimes being sieved to make the texture even smoother. For preserves, the fruit is also cooked with sugar (for a slightly shorter time), but whole or large pieces are often used and they more or less retain their shape.

Ingredients - Fruit and sugar are the basic ingredients and, depending on the recipe, natural or commercially prepared pectin or tartaric acid may be added. It is possible to buy a type of preserving sugar which contains a small proportion of fruit pectin and acid. Pectin occurs naturally in appreciable quantities in the skin or peel, seeds and cores of certain fruits such as apples and quinces (the latter are a particularly rich source). This sets when heated to the right temperature for the correct length of time (and no longer!). Some low-acid, low-pectin fruit jams and jellies do not set well, so one apple per 2lb / 1kg of fruit should be added or commercial pectin used (concentrated apple juice); otherwise you can use the special preserving sugar mentioned above.

Be sure to use the correct proportions of fruit and sugar. Sugar is the preserving agent and a jam (or preserve) must contain at least 65 per cent sugar; the recipes in this book have, of course, been devised so that sugar quantities vary according to the natural sugar content of the fruit. Jam which has too low a sugar content will grow a layer of mould on top; too much sugar may cause the jam to crystallize. In the first case, simply remove the mould and boil the jam for a few minutes. If crystallized, boil the jam, adding a little water or alcohol (brandy or liqueur or even wine). If you pot up the jam while it is still hot, all should be well (see below).

Cooking the jam - Start off by boiling fast to give the moisture content of the fruit a chance to evaporate, and skim off the foam or scum; then reduce the heat and stir very frequently so the fruit blends with the sugar. Cooking time will vary according to the type and quantity of fruit used. Some jams take only 20 minutes, but a few take as long as an hour or more. Try not to overcook as the jam will lose its colour and the gel may also be affected. You can find out if it is done by the following test: take some of the hot liquid in a wooden spoon, lift above the pan and then tilt the spoon over; if the liquid has almost reached setting point, it

will fall back into the pan in a single thin stream like honey and needs a little more cooking; if it comes away from the spoon in distinctly separate sheets or blobs, sliding off and leaving the surface of the spoon fairly clean, now is the time to take the pan off the heat and pour the jam into jars. Another way to test setting point is to place a teaspoon of the jam on a cold plate: if it sticks to it quickly with a well-defined edge (no watery surround), it is ready. Lastly, you can place a few drops of jam on a cold plate: after cooling, it should wrinkle when pushed with your finger if it is set. While testing for set, take the pan off the heat.

Filling and sealing the jars - As soon as they have reached setting point, jams and preserves can be transferred to jars while still hot. Warm the jars and, as soon as you have removed the pan from the heat, start filling them to within ½in / 1cm of their rims. Seal tightly straight away - the residual heat will carry out the sterilization for you; store in a dry place. You can wrap the jars in cloths to keep them hot longer; store when cool. This hot potting method is good for thin jams with a lower sugar content. Alternatively, you can wait until the jam is cold (but not set), when absolutely clean jars can be filled with the cold jam, sealed, labelled and stored in a cool, dry and dark spot.

Canning or bottling fruit in syrup

This is a very straightforward way of keeping fruit and simply entails packing clean, prepared fruit (whole or in pieces) into jars and covering with sugar syrup. Since the sugar is in a fairly weak solution, however, it will not be so effective in preserving the fruit as in the case of jam, so the sealed jars must be sterilized for a set time, depending on the type of fruit and the concentration of sugar in the syrup. See page 119 for the sterilizing method.

Canning or bottling fruit in alcohol

Use spirits or liqueurs with a high alcohol content whenever possible, since the juices of the fruit reduce the alcohol's strength. The process of osmosis will cause the less concentrated liquid, the fruit's moisture content, to seep out into the alcohol, and then gradually the mingled alcohol and juice will be re-absorbed by the fruit.

About one month after canning or bottling the fruit, you can add a sugar syrup to the jars: allow 1 generous cup / 9oz / 250g sugar, boiled with just enough water to moisten thoroughly for two minutes, for every 4½lb / 2kg fruit. Wait until the syrup is cold before pouring it into the jars. Not only will the fruit be sweeter, but the liquid in which it is preserved will carry less of an alcoholic punch.

Preserves and jams made with orchard and exotic fruits

Whether the fruit comes from nearby trees
or is imported, there is a tremendous variety
of raw material with which to make delicious preserves
with a high energy content.
Enjoy the results at breakfast time
or use to make genuine, home-made cakes and desserts.
Some of these preserves go very well
with boiled or roast meat and poultry.

Morello cherry jam

INGREDIENTS

- *6½lb / 3kg firm, ripe cherries (pitted/stoned)*
- *6½cups / 3lb 5oz / 1½kg preserving sugar*
- *1 lemon*
- *¼cup / 2fl oz / 50ml maraschino liqueur*
- *½cup / 4fl oz / 125ml water*

METHOD

Place the washed and pitted/stoned cherries in a bowl and sprinkle with the juice of the lemon and its finely grated peel (avoid using any of the bitter white pith).

Place the sugar and water in a preserving pan large enough to hold the cherries, and still leave plenty of room; bring to the boil and, once the sugar has dissolved, add the cherries.

Continue boiling gently, removing scum from time to time. Stir frequently with a wooden spoon. When the jam becomes thick and sticky or when a few drops are tested on a cold plate (when the plate is tipped they should run down it very slowly), remove the pan from the heat and stir in the maraschino. Transfer to prepared jam jars while still hot and seal tightly. Store in a cool, dark place.

Extra flavour can be imparted to the jam by adding a clove and a small piece of cinnamon bark to the cherries. Remove and discard spices before potting and sealing.

Pineapple jam

INGREDIENTS

- *4½lb / 2kg fresh pineapple chunks*
- *2 apples*
- *1 lemon*
- *4lb / 1.8kg preserving sugar*

METHOD

For easy peeling and coring of the pineapple, use a serrated knife to cut off both ends, and slice between the rows of 'eyes'; remove hard core with an apple corer or grapefruit knife; cut the hard skin off each slice. Peel and core the apples. Cut the apples and pineapple into fairly small pieces and place in a large bowl. Mix in the sugar and the juice and finely grated rind of the lemon. Cover and leave to stand for 5-6 hours.

Transfer to a large, deep saucepan or preserving pan and bring slowly to the boil, skimming and stirring with a wooden spoon.

Cook very gently until the jam reaches setting point. Transfer while hot to prepared jars and seal tightly. As soon as the jam is completely cold, store in a cool, dry place.

Make sure the pineapples are sound and not overripe – the flesh should be pale yellow and the leaves at the top should not be dry or withered.

Melon jam

Sweet-sour pineapple conserve

INGREDIENTS

1¼lb / 600g canned (drained) or fresh pineapple chunks
1⅓ cups / 11oz / 300g sugar
½ cup / 2 oz / 50g seedless white raisins/sultanas
1 tablespoon mustard powder
1 lemon
2-3 juniper berries
small piece cinnamon bark
2-3 dried hot red (chilli) peppers
3 cloves
1¼ cup / ½ pint / 300ml best quality white wine vinegar

METHOD

Place the vinegar and sugar in a large, heavy saucepan. Crush the juniper berries and wrap in a clean piece of cheesecloth or muslin with the cloves, cinnamon and peppers; fasten tightly and bring to a fast boil in the vinegar and sugar for 2-3 minutes.

Add the pineapple, mustard, the juice and very thin strips of rind (no pith) of the lemon, together with the washed, drained raisins/sultanas.

Bring to the boil again and cook very slowly, stirring frequently. After about 15 minutes, remove and discard the muslin bag of flavourings. When the conserve reaches setting point, remove from the heat and ladle into prepared jars at once. Seal tightly while hot.

When cold, store in a cool, dark cellar or cupboard.

The flavour of this conserve is reminiscent of the famous mustard fruits of Cremona: delicious in small quantities with all types of roast meat and poultry. Used sparingly, it will bring out the full flavour of the meat.

Cherry jam with honey

INGREDIENTS

2¼lb / 1kg pitted/stoned firm, ripe cherries
2⅓ cups / 1¾lb / 800g clear honey
1 juicy lemon (juice and pared rind)

METHOD

Place the washed, drained and pitted/stoned cherries in a large preserving pan or heavy saucepan with a large strip of lemon peel (no pith) and the honey.

Bring slowly to a gentle boil, removing any scum and stirring occasionally with a long-handled wooden spoon.

When the jam has reached the right consistency (test for setting), remove from the heat. Remove and discard the lemon peel and stir in the lemon juice.

Transfer the hot jam into jars and seal at once very tightly. Storage should be cool and dark.

This cherry and honey jam is both extremely wholesome and delicious (children love it). Spread on lightly toasted wholemeal bread, it makes a good breakfast.

Fig and brandy jam

INGREDIENTS

5½lb / 2½kg sound ripe figs
4½ cups / 2¼lb / 1kg preserving sugar
½ lemon
¼ cup / 2fl oz / 50ml brandy

METHOD

Trim the stalks from the figs and remove as much of the thin, glossy outer skin as will come off easily.

Cut into small pieces and place in a large non-aluminium saucepan; leave to stand for ¾-1 hour. Add the sugar and a few pieces of closely pared lemon peel, and bring to a slow boil while stirring continuously with a wooden spoon. Skim off any scum at intervals.

When the jam is thick enough (test as directed on pages 11-12), stir in the brandy and lemon juice.

Cook for a minute or two over moderate heat, stirring to make sure the jam does not stick to the bottom of the pan and burn.

Ladle the hot jam into jars and seal, making sure they are airtight. Store in a cool, dark place.

Late summer figs, either the brown or green-skinned varieties, are best for this jam as they are full of natural sugar.

Sharp lemon and apple conserve

INGREDIENTS

2¼lb / 1kg lemons
3¼lb / 1½kg peeled, cored and sliced apples
5¼ cups / 2lb 10oz / 1.2 kg preserving sugar
1 quart / 1¾ pints / 1 litre water
¼ cup / 2fl oz / 50ml brandy (optional)

METHOD

Place the apples in a large preserving pan.

Wash the lemons and wipe them dry. Cut lengthwise into quarters, removing pips and trimming both ends. Slice very finely, taking care to collect all the juice; add the lemons and juice to the apples as you slice them to prevent them discolouring. Add the water and sugar and bring slowly to the boil.

Remove any scum and cook, stirring frequently until all the water has evaporated and the jam turns to a thick, jelly-like consistency (test for setting).

Remove from the heat and add, if desired, the brandy or other liqueur (Grand Marnier, etc).

Pre-warm the jars before pouring in the hot jam. Seal hermetically at once and store in a cool, dark and dry place.

A very refreshing jam, not too sweet but with plenty of taste. The sharpness makes it ideal for fruit flans or tarts, or as part of special puddings and cakes.

Apple jam and Caramelized apple jam

Melon jam

INGREDIENTS

- *6½lb / 3kg melon(s)*
- *4½ cups / 2¼lb / 1kg sugar*
- *4 lemons*
- *½ cup / 4fl oz / 125ml brandy*
- *1½ quarts / generous 2½ pints / 1½ litres water*

METHOD

Scoop out the melon seeds and discard; scoop out all the flesh and weigh: this recipe calls for 4½lb / 2kg.

Place the melon flesh in a large, heavy saucepan, pour in the water and add the lemon juice and a few pieces of peel (without any of the white pith attached). Bring slowly to the boil and then simmer gently for about 30 minutes, until the melon takes on a transparent look.

Add the sugar and continue cooking, stirring frequently with a wooden spoon, until the jam reaches the correct consistency (test on a tilted plate).

Stir in the brandy and leave to cool completely before spooning into absolutely clean jars. Seal tightly and store in a dry, dark cupboard or storeroom.

Choose melons with plenty of flavour and scent, and with firm, ripe flesh. Choose late summer and early autumn ripening varieties, not forced or greenhouse-grown melons. Cantaloupe melons are the best for jam.

Pear preserve

INGREDIENTS

- *2¼lb / 1kg sound, ripe pears*
- *2 cups / 1lb / 500g preserving sugar*
- *2 cups / 16 fl oz / 450ml water*
- *1 lemon*
- *1 tablespoon marc or liqueur*

METHOD

Buy or pick the pears before they are quite ripe and set one aside to test for ripeness; it should not feel soft but should be very juicy when cut. Peel and core the pears and drop into a large bowl of cold water acidulated with the lemon juice.

Drain the pears and place in a preserving pan, adding the sugar and water. Bring slowly to the boil while stirring. When tender, break the fruit up by stirring well with a stainless steel whisk. Continue boiling gently until the preserve is thick enough.

Transfer the hot mixture into prepared jars and sprinkle the surface of each jar of preserve with a few drops of pear marc, liqueur or brandy to add more flavour. Seal tightly and keep in a dark, dry place.

The best pears for this preserve are late summer pears; late autumn or winter ripening pears are best for jams and compotes.

Spiced pear preserve

INGREDIENTS

- *6½lb / 3kg firm, dense-fleshed cooking pears*
- *2 quarts / 3½ pints / 2 litres white wine*
- *1 cup / 8fl oz / 225 ml water*
- *4½ cups / 2¼ lb / 1kg sugar*
- *2 lemons*
- *1 orange (peel only)*
- *7-8 cloves*
- *generous pinch ground cinnamon*
- *generous ½ cup / 7oz / 200g clear honey*
- *2-3 tablespoons English mustard powder*

METHOD

Wash, dry and peel the pears, quarter and core them, dropping them immediately into a preserving pan containing the wine, water, lemon juice and grated rind and the thinly pared orange peel (no pith).

Add all the remaining ingredients and bring to a gentle boil, stirring and skimming at intervals.

When the preserve has reached the required thick consistency, remove from the heat and transfer to wide-necked jars while still very hot. Keep in a dry, dark storage space.

With its subtle 'kick' this preserve makes an ideal accompaniment to boiled or poached meat, poultry and to roast game. The amount of mustard can be increased it you want a more pronounced flavour.

Plum preserve

INGREDIENTS

- *6½lb / 3kg ripe, sound plums, greengages or damsons (pitted/stoned)*
- *7 cups / 3½lb / 1.6kg sugar*
- *1 lemon*

METHOD

Wash the plums, cut them into fairly large pieces and place in a preserving pan with the lemon juice, a few strips of peel and the sugar. Stir and bring slowly to the boil; cook gently while stirring and removing any scum at frequent intervals.

When the preserve has reached the correct consistency, remove from the heat and pour into warmed jars, sealing tightly. Store in a dry, dark spot.

The best plums for this method of preserving are greengages (originally known as 'Reine Claude') or damsons. They are perfect for filling flans and tarts.

Grape jelly

INGREDIENTS

- *7¾lb / 3½kg grapes*
- *7 cups / 3½ lb / 1.6kg sugar*
- *1 lemon*

METHOD

Wash the grapes and detach from their stalks. Place in a preserving pan, add the sugar and a few drops of lemon juice.

Mix well and bring to the boil. Simmer, removing scum and stirring frequently. As the grape skins rise to the surface, skim them off with a slotted spoon, pressing them against the spoon with a fork to squeeze out all the juice, letting it drop back into the pan. Discard the skins.

Continue cooking until the preserve reaches setting point. Remove from the heat and spoon into jars.

Seal tightly and keep in a dry, dark place.

This grape preserve is best mixed with a slightly more tart jam, such as the plum recipe on page 20, as it can be a little too sweet.

Old-fashioned grape preserve

INGREDIENTS

- *3¼-3½lb / approx 1½kg very ripe, firm grapes*
- *2½-2¾lb / approx 1.2kg small pears*
- *scant cup / 7oz / 200g sugar*
- *1 lemon*
- *1 pinch ground cinnamon*

METHOD

Wash the grapes thoroughly under cold running water; pick off the individual grapes, place in a fine hair sieve and press out the juice (they should yield about 5 cups / 2-2¼ pints / 1-1¼ litres juice). Bring the juice to the boil in a stainless steel or copper pan and reduce to about 2½-3 cups / 1-1¼ pints / 600-700ml in volume. As the liquid boils and evaporates, skim and stir when necessary. While the grape juice is reducing, wash and peel the pears; cut into quarters or smaller slices, remove the cores and have them ready just as the liquid has reduced sufficiently so they will not have time to discolour. This quantity should net about 2¼lb / 1kg pear slices.

Add the pears to the liquid, with the sugar, lemon juice, a few pieces of lemon peel and the cinnamon. Continue simmering while stirring until the preserve is thick enough. Remove from heat; pour into warmed jars while boiling hot.

Seal the jars tightly without delay and make sure they are stored in a dry, dark cupboard or storeroom.

Children are particularly partial to the intense sweetness of this preserve, spread on toasted slices of bread or crackers or used to sweeten hot or cold drinks.

Apricot jam

INGREDIENTS

10lb / 4kg sound, ripe apricots
4lb / 1.8kg preserving sugar
1 lemon

METHOD

Rinse the apricots quickly to get rid of any traces of fungicide, drain and remove the pits/stones. Chop half the apricots into small pieces and tip into the preserving pan. Sieve the remaining half, add to the pan and sprinkle with the juice of the lemon and a pinch of its grated peel.

Place the pan over a moderate heat and bring to a gentle boil; cook for about 2 minutes, removing scum.

Add the sugar and allow to return to the boil; cook slowly, stirring frequently (do not try to remove any more scum), until the mixture starts to thicken.

When setting point is reached, remove immediately from the heat and transfer straightaway into prepared pots, sealing tightly. Store in a cool, dark place.

You can put this jam to all sorts of uses. Try diluting it slightly, stirring in a little white wine while heating; it can then be used as a glaze for fruit flans, tarts and pastries.

Pineapple and kiwi fruit jam

INGREDIENTS

4 kiwi fruit
2¼lb / 1kg fresh pineapple chunks
5 cups / 2½lb / 1.1kg sugar
1 lemon
1 vanilla pod

METHOD

Peel the kiwi fruit, mash the flesh with a fork and push through a fine sieve into a bowl; mix in the pineapple cubes and the sugar; leave to stand overnight or for 8-10 hours.

Tip the fruit and juices into the preserving pan, adding the vanilla pod and lemon juice. Bring the mixture slowly to the boil, stirring constantly with a wooden spoon. Allow 30 minutes' cooking time from the moment boiling point is reached; remove scum at frequent intervals.

Ladle the hot jam into sterilized jars and leave to cool before sealing tightly. Store in a cool, dark place.

This jam is exceptionally rich in vitamin C, as the vitamin content of one kiwi fruit equals that of about 10 lemons (or 105mg per 100g of fruit); one kiwi fruit a day would give a child the daily requirement of vitamin C.

Apple and orange jam

Apple and orange jam

INGREDIENTS

- *7-8 juicy oranges*
- *½lb / 200g peeled, cored, sliced apples*
- *2½ cups / 1¼lb / 600g sugar*

METHOD

Pare off the rind of two oranges, taking care to leave behind all the white pith, which is very bitter. Chop quite finely. Peel all the remaining oranges and remove all traces of pith from each orange. Cut the oranges into pieces, discarding the seeds and the fibrous strips from the thin edge of each segment. Place the flesh and juice in a non-aluminium saucepan and add the apples (these provide extra pectin to ensure a good set) and the sugar.

Bring the mixture to the boil and keep it boiling for 5 minutes without skimming.

Once the apples are cooked, remove from the heat and put the mixture through a sieve or food mill (or a processor).

Return to the pan, stir in the chopped peel and simmer slowly, removing the scum now and then. When the jam has thickened to the consistency of honey, remove from the heat and ladle the hot jam into jars. Seal tightly and keep in a cool, dark place.

Apart from its uses as a normal jam, this is particularly good as a filling for doughnuts, fritters and baked puddings.

Orange and lemon marmalade

INGREDIENTS

- *2¼lb / 1kg Seville (bitter) or sweet oranges*
- *2¼lb / 1kg lemons*
- *6 cups / 3lb / 1.4kg sugar*

METHOD *(see illustrated instructions on page 186)*

Pare off the peel of the oranges and lemons thinly. Peel off all the bitter white pith covering the fruit. Chop the flesh coarsely, weigh and place in a non-metallic preserving pan.

Cut the peel into thin, short strips (the peel can be grated when removing from the fruit but remember to avoid any pith) and add to the pan together with the sugar.

Bring to the boil and then simmer, stirring with a wooden spoon and skimming. When the marmalade reaches setting point, remove from the heat and pour into jars while still hot. Seal at once and store in a cool, dry place.

Try stirring small quantities of this jam into apple purée and serving it as a sauce for spit-roasted or oven-roasted game.

Banana jam

INGREDIENTS

2¼lb / 1kg (peeled weight) bananas
3¼ cups / 1lb 10oz / 750g sugar
1 lemon
½ cup / 4fl oz / 125ml water

METHOD

Boil the sugar and water in a large, heavy saucepan for 3-4 minutes. Sieve the peeled bananas into a large bowl containing the lemon juice. Mix quickly and then add to the sugar syrup in the pan while it is still hot. Time is of the essence if the bananas are not to discolour.

Boil the jam gently, stirring all the time as it can stick and burn very easily.

As soon as the jam has thickened sufficiently, pour it into warmed jars and sprinkle a pinch of extra sugar on the surface of the hot jam before sealing tightly and sterilizing for about 10 minutes (see page 119). Keep in a cool, dark place.

Banana jam is high in nutritional value but will only keep well if perfectly sound, ripe fruit have been chosen and great care taken in its preparation.

Persimmon jam

INGREDIENTS

4½lb / 2kg very ripe persimmons
1 dessert apple
1 lemon
6¼ cups / 3lb 2oz / 1.4kg preserving sugar
small piece vanilla pod
¼ cup / 2fl oz / 50ml liqueur

METHOD

Wash the persimmons, pull off the stalk and calyx and squeeze the soft, gelatinous flesh out of the skins by hand, straight into the preserving pan.

Peel, core and chop the apple and add to the persimmons together with the juice and the lemon peel (avoid any pith).

Bring to the boil and simmer for 3-4 minutes, skimming off the scum. Remove from heat; sieve and return the purée to the pan.

Add the sugar and piece of vanilla pod. Bring to a gentle boil and remove all the scum as it surfaces. Continue stirring and skimming until the jam is thick enough. Remove from the heat, stir in the liqueur of your choice and pot while still hot. Keep cool and dark.

Use to sweeten hot drinks such as tea, and tisanes. If Sharon fruit are used, choose firm fruits with a brownish tinge under the skin. Real persimmons (kakis) must be overripe and translucent.

Citron marmalade

Citron marmalade

INGREDIENTS

3¼lb / 1½kg ripe, juicy citrons
4½cups / 2¼lb / 1kg sugar
¼ cup / 2fl oz / 50ml rum
1 quart / 1¾ pints / 1 litre water

METHOD *(see illustrated instructions on page 187)*

Wash the citrons, cut lengthwise in half and leave to stand in a large bowlful of cold water for two days, changing the water every 12 hours to lessen the bitter taste.

Place the drained citron halves in a large heavy saucepan, add enough fresh water to just cover and cook very gently until the rind is very soft and tender (a lengthy process). Drain off the liquid and cut the citrons into small pieces.

Make a sugar syrup by heating the sugar in the water over a low heat until completely dissolved; add the chopped citrons and cook for 20 minutes, stirring continuously with a wooden spoon. Turn off the heat, leave to cool and then stir in the rum.

Spoon the citron marmalade into prepared glass jars, seal tightly and store in a cool, dark place.

The pleasantly sharp taste of citrons makes this an enjoyable, easily digested jam, even when eaten on its own by the spoonful.

Cherry jam

INGREDIENTS

11lb / 5kg pitted/stoned cherries
6½lb / 3kg sugar
about 12 small cherry tree leaves (optional)

METHOD

Wash the cherries, remove the stalks and pits/stones. Transfer the cherries into a large preserving pan and stir in the sugar.

Bring slowly to a gentle boil, skimming if necessary. Stir at very frequent intervals with a long-handled wooden spoon as the jam cooks to prevent it sticking and burning on the bottom of the pan. If a few drops will set on a cold plate when tested, it is time to remove from the heat and ladle the hot jam at once into ready warmed jars. Place a cherry tree leaf or two in the middle of each pot of jam.

Make sure the jars are hermetically sealed before putting them away in a cool, dark place.

Equally delicious on toast, as a filling for tartlets or served as a dessert with or without cream or ice-cream.

Quince and sugar-beet jam

INGREDIENTS

6½lb / 3kg very ripe, sound quinces
2-3 white sugar-beet
4½ cups / 2¼lb / 1kg sugar

METHOD

Peel and core the quinces; cut into small pieces (this should yield about 4½lb / 2kg flesh) and place in a preserving pan.

Peel and chop the sugar-beets and add to the quinces; pour in enough water to cover.

Bring the mixture to the boil and then cook slowly over a very gentle heat, stirring all the time until the jam reaches setting point. Make sure you scrape the bottom of the pan with the wooden spoon when mixing or the jam will stick. Half way through cooking, add the sugar.

Remove from the heat, transfer into jars and seal tightly. Store in a cool, dry place.

This dense, highly flavoured jam is ideal as a filling for fritters and doughnuts or dumplings.

Mango jam

INGREDIENTS

2¼lb / 1kg mango flesh
4½ cup / 2¼lb / 1kg sugar
1 vanilla pod
1 cup / 8fl oz / 225ml water
1 cup / 8 fl ow/225ml rum

METHOD

Heat the sugar and water together in a large preserving pan or heavy saucepan and cook over low heat until the sugar has completely dissolved.

Add the diced mango flesh to the sugar syrup, followed by the crumbled vanilla pod. Simmer for 30 minutes, removing scum frequently with a wooden spoon.

Leave to cool slightly.

Place a disc of waxed paper, dipped in rum, on the surface of each jar of jam. Make sure the jars are airtight when sealed.

Keep in a dry, dark place.

As mango is rich in vitamin A and D and in mineral salts such as iron, this is a very nutritious jam.

Apple jam

INGREDIENTS

5½lb / 2½kg apples

5¼ cups / 2lb 10 oz / 1.2kg sugar

1 lemon

METHOD

Peel, core and slice the apples into a large bowl. Sprinkle with the lemon juice to prevent discolouration. Transfer to a large preserving pan and add the sugar.

Bring to the boil and cook slowly, stirring and removing any scum; while they are cooking, press the apples against the base and sides of the pan to reduce them to a purée. When the jam has reached the correct consistency, leave to cool and then spoon into absolutely clean, dry jars.

If the apples are a very crisp cooking variety, cut into small dice before cooking.

If you like a more distinct lemony taste, stir in a little grated lemon rind before potting – be sure to avoid the pith, as this is unpleasantly bitter. Just the thing for your next Apfelstrudel.

Apple and chocolate conserve

INGREDIENTS

2¼lb / 1kg Reinette apples, peeled and cored

3 cups / 1¼lb / 600g sugar

scant ½ cup / 1½ oz / 40g cocoa powder (unsweetened)

1 lemon

small piece vanilla pod

METHOD

Pour the lemon juice and half its rind, finely grated, into a large saucepan; add the diced or sliced apples and mix well to prevent discolouration.

Mix the sugar with very good quality cocoa or bitter baking chocolate in a separate bowl and then stir well into the apples, making sure there are no lumps. Add the crumbled vanilla pod and set over a low heat. Once the mixture has come to the boil, lower the heat and cook gently, stirring continuously with a wooden spoon.

When the apples are completely cooked and tender, remove from the heat and put through a fine sieve, vegetable mill (with the smallest measurement disc) or food processor.

Return the rich brown purée to the pan, bring up to a very gentle boil; do not skim.

When the mixture is thick enough (the apples will ensure it sets well even if it looks rather moist), ladle the hot jam into warmed jars to within ¼in / 1cm of the rim. Make sure the lids are airtight and store in a cool, dark place.

Spread on fresh crusty bread at breakfast time or use as an unusual filling for pies or dessert pastries.

Caramelized apple jam

INGREDIENTS

- *5lb / 2.3kg apples*
- *4½ cups / 2¼lb / 1kg sugar*
- *1 lemon*
- *¼ cup / 2fl oz / 50ml brandy*
- *¼ cup / 2fl oz / 50ml water*

METHOD

Wash the apples, peel, core and dice; sprinkle with the lemon juice to prevent them turning brown. Mix 1¾ cups / 14oz / 300g of the sugar with the water in a large, heavy saucepan and bring to a slow boil (if cooking on gas, make sure the flames do not lick the sides of the pan or the caramel will burn round the edge). When the caramel is a pale golden brown, remove at once from the heat and waste no time in stirring in the apples (beware of scalding steam at this point).

Once the apples are well mixed into the caramel, add the remaining sugar. Return to a low heat and bring very slowly back to boiling point, stirring all the time. When the apples are done, turn into a fine hair sieve and return the purée to the pan. If it is very thick, boil for just a minute more: if it seems a bit too liquid, reduce by cooking longer. Turn off the heat, add the brandy and spoon into the jars straightaway.

Seal tightly and keep in a cool, dark place.

Make sure your caramel is quite pale because the sugar goes on cooking after it has been taken off the heat and can burn and turn bitter in no time. Adding the apples and stirring stops the cooking process.

Pear jam

INGREDIENTS

- *11lb / 5kg sound, ripe dessert pears*
- *11 cups / 5½lb / 2½kg sugar*
- *1 lemon*
- *2 cups / 18 fl oz 500 ml water*

METHOD

Peel and core the pears; slice them straight into a large preserving pan. Add the juice and grated rind of the lemon and the water. Stir and bring slowly to the boil; then cook gently, stirring and skimming frequently. The pears should be cooked after 10 minutes. Remove from the heat and push through a fine sieve, foodmill or processor. Return the purée to the pan, stir in the sugar and bring gently back to a slow boil, stirring all the time.

When the jam has reached the correct consistency, it should be poured, while still hot, into warmed jars. Seal well and keep in cool, dry storage.

Autumn and early winter ripening pears produce the best results for this recipe – use the summer pears for preserves.

Quince and sugar-beet jam

Peach jam

INGREDIENTS

11lb / 5kg sound, ripe peaches
5½lb / 2½kg sugar
2 lemons
approx 12 tender, young peach leaves

METHOD

Wash the peaches well, pit/stone and chop coarsely into a preserving pan. Sprinkle with the juice of the lemons and add a few pieces of thinly pared peel.

Bring slowly to the boil, removing scum and stirring. Cook gently for 5 minutes, and when the peaches are done, remove from the heat and sieve or put through a vegetable mill (or processor).

Return the purée to the preserving pan and add the sugar. Bring to the boil again and cook gently while stirring continuously with a wooden spoon – this jam sticks and burns on the bottom of the pan very easily.

When the jam is thick enough, turn off the heat and pour into warmed jars, sealing tightly without delay.

Store in a cool, dark cellar or storeroom.

The delicate flavour can best be appreciated when spread on fresh bread, on top of a little unsalted butter.

Damson jam

INGREDIENTS

8¾lb / 4kg damsons
4lb / 1.8kg sugar
1 lemon
1 cup / 8fl oz / 225 ml water

METHOD

Wash the damsons very thoroughly under the cold tap. Cut them in half, remove the pit/stone and stalk and reweigh: you should end up with about 6½lb / 3kg net weight. Place the damsons in a preserving pan, sprinkle with the lemon juice, add a few pieces of lemon peel and the water. Bring to a slow boil and cook for about 5 minutes, or until the damsons are mushy.

Remove from the heat and put through a fine sieve or vegetable mill. Return the purée to the pan, stir in the sugar and continue cooking, while stirring, until the jam is sufficiently thick. Skim when necessary.

Turn off the heat and ladle into prepared jars, filling them to within ¼ in / 1cm from the rim. Place the lids on the jars, making sure they are airtight, and keep cool and dark.

Other varieties of firm, full-flavoured, dark-skinned plums can be used for this recipe.

Jams and preserves made with wild fruits

In summer and early autumn
a rich store of wild fruits awaits
anyone who cares to pick them from shady woods
and wayside hedgerows once the early morning sun
has dried their sprinkling of dew.
They make wonderful, unusual preserves and jams.

Cape gooseberry (physalis) jam

INGREDIENTS

2¼lb / 1kg ripe Chinese Lantern fruit (Physalis alkekengi) or Cape gooseberries

1lb / 500g sugar

1½ cups / 12fl oz / 350ml water

METHOD

Remove the berries from their casings; wash and dry. Place the sugar and water in a large, heavy-bottomed saucepan and heat to make a sugar syrup, cooking over a low heat until the sugar has completely dissolved; boil gently for 10 minutes more before adding the fruit, and simmer until the jam is thick enough to set.

Transfer the jam into jars, seal well and store in a dry, dark place.

This preserve goes well with roast lamb or mutton, being somewhat sharp and acidulated; it is also excellent as a filling for tartlets and cookies. These fruit are also called ground cherries in the USA The wild, temperate-climate Chinese Lantern fruit (Physalis alkekengi) are redder and sharper in taste.

Sweet chestnut and brandy preserve

INGREDIENTS

3¼-3½lb / 1½kg Spanish (sweet) chestnuts

4½ cups / 2¼lb / 1kg sugar

1¼ cups / ½ pint / 300ml water

1 bay leaf

pinch fennel seeds (or 1 fennel stalk)

pinch grated lemon peel

pinch grated orange peel

¼ cup / 2fl oz / 50ml brandy for every 2¼lb / 1kg of chestnut purée

METHOD

Boil the chestnuts in plenty of water together with the fennel (seeds or stalk) and the bay leaf. When they are done, peel while still hot, and mix with the sugar, water and grated orange and lemon rind (avoid the white pith).

Transfer to a preserving pan and boil gently, stirring very well as the chestnuts will tend to stick to the bottom of the pan; break up the chestnuts as you stir.

Continue cooking and stirring over a very low heat until the chestnuts have turned into a thick purée (which need not be absolutely smooth); remove from the heat and stir in the brandy.

Pot while still hot, trickling a thin layer of brandy over the surface in each jar. Keep in a dry, dark place after sealing tightly.

Choose large, firm chestnuts. Once opened, this preserve does not keep well – a thin layer of mould may appear after a short time – so finish each jar as soon as possible.

Jam tarts

Wild strawberry preserve

INGREDIENTS

6½lb / 3kg wild strawberries
7½ cups / 3¾lb / 1.7kg sugar
1 lemon
¼ cup / 2fl oz / 50ml maraschino
1 cup / 8fl oz / 225ml water

METHOD

The strawberries should be firm and ripe and need not be rinsed unless they are gritty or mud-spattered; place them dry in a bowl and sprinkle with the lemon juice and finely grated peel.

Boil the water and sugar until the sugar has dissolved and cook for 3-4 minutes, making sure it does not colour at all. Pour straight over the strawberries, stir and leave to stand for 1 hour.

Pour the strawberries and syrup into a preserving pan, bring slowly up to a gentle boil and cook while stirring. When the preserve has reached setting point, turn off the heat, stir in the maraschino and pour into jars while still hot. Make sure the lids are airtight and keep under cool, dark storage conditions.

Cultivated strawberries can also be used, but use only those picked in high summer, not the forced or late varieties. Rum can be used instead of maraschino.

Raspberry preserve

INGREDIENTS

2¼lb / 1kg firm, ripe raspberries
3 cups / 1¼lb / 600g sugar
1 lemon

METHOD

If possible, pick the raspberries first thing in the morning, never during the hottest time of the day; choose sound, very ripe berries. Rinse briefly in cold water and drain well.

Dry on paper towels if necessary. Place in a bowl and sprinkle with the sugar and lemon juice.

Leave to stand for at least 2 hours; drain off all their juice and reduce it to a fairly thick syrup, preferably in a copper saucepan or preserving pan.

When the juice has reduced to half its original volume, add the raspberries and cook while stirring and skimming until the preserve has reached setting point.

Remove from the heat and pour the hot mixture into warmed jars. Make sure the lids are airtight to keep the delicious aroma of the raspberries intact, and store in a dry, dark place.

Handle the raspberries as little as possible before they are transferred to the pan because they deteriorate rapidly, especially on a hot day.

Blueberry/bilberry preserve

INGREDIENTS

2¼lb / 1kg wild blueberries/ bilberries
1lb / 500g sugar
1 lemon

METHOD

Wild bilberries, whortleberries or blueberries seem to have more flavour and aroma than almost any other wild berry; they make marvellous jam. If they are not dirty or dusty, do not wash them; if you must, do so very gently and quickly. Pick out any leaves or stalks.

Place them in a large bowl, cover with the sugar, sprinkle with the juice and grated rind of the lemon. Leave to stand for up to half a day, covered with a cloth.

Transfer to a preserving pan and bring to a very gentle boil, stirring and skimming frequently – the mixture is apt to stick and burn on the bottom of the pan.

When the preserve is thick and glossy and sets when tested, turn off the heat. Ladle into warmed jars while hot and make sure they are tightly sealed. Choose a cool, dark place for storage.

Diluted with a little brandy, this makes a wonderful sauce to go with roast turkey or duck.

Blackberry preserve

INGREDIENTS

4½lb / 2kg blackberries
5¼ cups / 2lb 10 oz / 1.2kg sugar
2 lemons
½ cup / 4 fl oz / 125ml water

METHOD

Choose sound, ripe wild blackberries and wash well in cold water or, better still, in white cooking wine. Leave to stand in the water or wine if they have a lot of insects on them. Drain well and dry on paper towels.

Bring the sugar and water to the boil in a large pan and cook over a low heat for 2-3 minutes. Pour the blackberries into the sugar syrup, stir well and simmer for 5-10 minutes. Ideally, the heat should now be turned off and the blackberries left to stand for at least half a day.

When this time is up, add the grated rind of one lemon. Return to the boil and cook while stirring and skimming. As soon as the preserve is thick enough, remove from the heat and stir in the juice of both lemons.

Pour into jam jars and seal tightly. Keep in a dry, dark place.

Excellent as a sauce poured over vanilla ice-cream or a fruit sorbet.

Red summertime preserve

INGREDIENTS

2¼lb / 1kg bilberries or blueberries
2¼lb / 1kg raspberries or loganberries
2¼lb / 1kg strawberries
1lb / 500g redcurrants
1lb / 500g black or Morello cherries
6½lb / 3kg sugar
generous cup / 9fl oz / 250ml water
1 lemon

METHOD

Rinse the fruit briefly under cold running water. Take the redcurrants and cherries off their stalks and pit / stone the latter; hull the strawberries.

Make a heavy sugar syrup in a large preserving pan by boiling the sugar and water gently for 3-4 minutes. When it is ready, pour in the fruit, starting with the firmest - the cherries.

Simmer for a few minutes before adding the next batch of fruit, adding the most tender - probably the raspberries - last.

Cook gently, stirring with a wooden spoon and removing scum if necessary.

Check if the preserve has thickened sufficiently by testing a few drops on a plate to see if they gel.

Remove from the heat; pour in the lemon juice, stir and ladle into warmed jars, sealing at once.

Store in a dark, dry place.

A delicious reminder of the height of summer when used in flans, fruit pies, trifles, ice-cream desserts and added to fruit salads.

Chestnut and rum jam

INGREDIENTS

3¼-3½lb / 1½kg Spanish (sweet) chestnuts
3½ cups / 1¾lb / 800g sugar
a few orange peel parings
a few lemon peel parings
¼ cup / 2fl oz / 50ml rum for each 2¼lb / 1kg of chestnut purée
scant cup / 7fl oz / 200ml water

METHOD

Boil the chestnuts in their skins in plenty of water, together with the parings of orange and lemon (no pith).

When they are done, drain, peel off the hard outer and thin inner skins while still hot and sieve or put through a vegetable mill straightaway. Weigh the purée (you should have at least 2¼lb / 1kg). Transfer to a large saucepan and stir in the sugar and water.

Bring to the boil and cook slowly while stirring and skimming. When the jam is thick enough, add the appropriate quantity of rum. Turn off the heat and spoon straight into warmed jars. Seal well and place in dry, dark storage.

Dried chestnuts can be used for this jam. Allow 1¾lb / 800g dried weight and leave to soak in cold water for at least half a day. Boil in the normal way, adding a generous pinch of salt to the water as well as the citrus parings. Reserve a scant cup / 7fl oz / 200ml of this water to add to the cooked, sieved chestnuts. A more expensive version of the recipe, but it will save a lot of work.

Cornelian cherry (cornel) jam

INGREDIENTS

- 3¼lb / 1½kg fully ripe cornelian cherries
- 1⅓ cups / 10 oz / 300g sugar
- generous ¼ cup / 3½oz / 100g clear honey
- ½ lemon
- 2 apples
- pinch ground cinnamon
- 2 cups / 18fl oz / 500 ml dry white wine

METHOD

Remove the stalks of the cornelian cherries (or cornels) and place them in a bowl of cold water to rinse. Drain well and transfer to a large preserving pan with the white wine, a few pieces of lemon peel and the two peeled, cored and sliced apples. Cornelian cherries are cooked whole; there is no need to pit/stone them at this stage.

Bring slowly to a gentle boil, stirring and skimming. When the cornels are tender and pulpy, remove from the heat and put through a fine sieve, letting the thin purée drop back into the pan (there should be about 2¼lb / 1kg of it). Add the sugar, honey, juice of the half lemon and the cinnamon.

Return to a slow boil and continue cooking while stirring until the jam has thickened (it should be a little less dense than usual).

Remove from the heat and pour the hot jam into jars. Seal tightly and store in a dry, dark and well-ventilated place.

This will go well with boiled and roast meat and feathered game; the consistency is closer to a sauce than to a jam.

Jujube jelly

INGREDIENTS

- 2¼lb / 1kg ripe jujubes
- 3 cups / 1¼lb / 600g sugar
- 1 lemon
- 1 cup / 8fl oz / 225ml water

METHOD

Wash and trim the jujubes, cut lengthwise in half and place in a saucepan with the water, lemon juice and two pieces of lemon peel. Cook until tender and then sieve.

Return the purée to the pan and boil gently until the jelly reaches setting point (test as usual by placing a drop of jam on a cold plate and seeing whether it gels as it cools). Remove from the heat and pour the hot jelly into warmed jars. Make sure the lids are airtight and then keep in a dry, dark cupboard.

An unusual and exotic jelly with a distinctive taste which is said to be good for the digestion.

Blueberry and blackberry jam

INGREDIENTS

1lb / 500g blueberries/bilberries or whortleberries
1lb / 500g wild blackberries
3 cups / 1¼lb / 600g sugar
approx ½ bottle white cooking wine
½ cup / 4fl oz / 125ml water

METHOD

Pick over the blueberries/bilberries and blackberries and then rinse in a bowl in the white wine. Drain well and transfer to a large, heavy saucepan, adding the water. Cook the fruit over a low heat for about 15 minutes, stirring from time to time.

Once the fruit has simmered, add the sugar and continue cooking until the jam reaches setting point (test a few drops on a cold plate to see if they gel).

Once the jam is ready, transfer at once into warmed jars and seal immediately. Store in a dry, dark place.

Pick a few slightly underripe blackberries as well: they will improve the setting qualities of the jam. This mixed fruit recipe makes a delicious addition to sundaes and cold creamy rice desserts like Pears Condé. Or try folding it into whipped cream or crème chantilly.

Sorb apple jam

INGREDIENTS

2¼lb / 1kg peeled sorb apples
4½ cups / 2¼lb / 1kg sugar
1 lemon

METHOD

Make sure you have the correct net weight of sorb apples after peeling them; place in a heavy saucepan and stir in the sugar, lemon juice and a small piece of peel. Cook at a gentle boil, stirring frequently with a wooden spoon.

When the jam reaches setting point (a drop placed on a cold plate should trickle very slowly down the plate when tilted), turn off the heat and ladle the hot jam into warm jars.

Seal the jars immediately. Store in a well-ventilated, cool, dark place.

This fruit is rarely seen, though the tree grows well in temperate climates; this full-flavoured, tasty jam can be used to flavour ice-cream and as a dessert topping.

Preserves and jams made with garden fruits and flowers

The subtle yet pervasive scent of rose petals
and other perfumed flowers
can lend an exquisite, unusual aroma
to preserves for special occasions
and discerning palates.

Rose petal and apple preserve

Orange flower and apple preserve

INGREDIENTS

4½lb / 2kg dessert apples (Reinette)

¼lb / 100g fresh orange flowers or 1 teaspoon orange flower water

5¼ cups / 2lb 10oz / 1.2kg sugar

generous ½ cup / 7oz / 200g clear acacia honey

1 lemon

generous cup / 9fl oz / 250ml water

METHOD

Peel the apples and chop coarsely into a preserving pan; add the lemon juice and grated rind.

If fresh flowers are used, bring the water to the boil, throw in the flowers (rinse them first), stir and turn off the heat. Leave to stand for about 30 minutes. Strain through cheesecloth placed in a sieve into the pan, stir into the apples, cover and leave to stand for 30 minutes more. Bring to a gentle boil, stirring and skimming. When the apples are cooked, sieve them and return the purée to the pan. (If orange flower water is used, stir in at this point.) Add the sugar and honey, return to the boil and cook until as thick as honey.

Do not cook this jam too fast or for too long – it tends to crystallize sooner than other jams. Pot up while still hot, seal tightly and keep in a cool, dark place.

Used for exotic desserts and fruit puddings. Failing orange flower water (from chemists or high-class grocers), use essential oil of sweet orange or mandarin.

Rose petal and apple preserve

INGREDIENTS

4½lb / 2kg apples

1lb / 500g fresh, highly scented red rose petals

generous 6 cups / 3lb / 1.4kg sugar

1 lemon

generous cup / 9fl oz / 250ml water

METHOD

Peel and chop the apples into a preserving pan. Sprinkle with the lemon juice and grated peel. Wash the rose petals in cold water, drain, nip off the yellow tips and stir into the apples. Pour in the water, cover and leave to stand for 30 minutes.

Bring to the boil and cook slowly while stirring and removing any scum. When the apples are done, take the pan off the heat and push the contents through a fine mesh sieve. Return the purée to the pan, stir in the sugar and bring slowly back to the boil while stirring. Once the preserve has become as thick as honey, take it off the heat (it tends to crystallize easily). Pour while hot into jam jars, seal at once and keep in a cool, dark place.

The versatile rose petal is, of course, used widely in perfume and cosmetic manufacture, but has been used in cooking since ancient times. Your garden roses (rosa indaca) are the best; failing this, triple-strength rose water (1½ teaspoonfuls) and colouring could be used.

Mint and apple jam

Chinese rose petal and fruit jam

INGREDIENTS

2¼lb / 1kg sound, ripe peaches
2¼lb / 1kg plums
5¾ cups / 2lb 14oz / 1.3kg sugar
7-10oz / 200-300g fresh, scented rose petals
1 lemon
pinch salt

METHOD

Pinch off the yellow pointed ends of the rose petals, place in a colander and lower into lightly salted boiling water, stirring to immerse all the petals. Drain and then refresh under cold running water; drain well, remove from the colander and pat dry with paper towels.

Spread the petals on a plate, sprinkle with generous ½ cup / 5oz / 150g of the sugar and the lemon juice. Leave for 2 hours. Prepare the peaches and plums: wash, dry, peel, pit/stone, chop into small pieces and place in pan. Add the remaining sugar, stir and leave to stand for 1 hour. Chop the prepared rose petals and stir into the pan contents.

Bring the fruit very slowly to the boil and cook gently, stirring and removing scum. As soon as setting point is reached, remove from the heat, pour the hot jam into warm jars and seal tightly. Store in a dark, dry place.

Full-flavoured and fleshy Burbank or Golden Drop plums are best for this recipe.

Elderberry jam

INGREDIENTS

6½lb / 3kg elderberries
10½ cups / 5¼lb / 2.4kg sugar
1 lemon
1¼ cups / 10fl oz / 300ml water

METHOD

Pick the bunches of elderberries when they are fully ripe – a purplish black, in late summer or early autumn.

Pick the berries off their stalks, rinse in cold water, drain and spread out to dry briefly. Place in the preserving pan with the sugar, a small piece of lemon peel, a few drops of lemon juice and the water. Bring to the boil, stirring with a wooden spoon and skimming when necessary. Boil gently until setting point is reached, remove from the heat and ladle the hot jam into warmed jars. Seal the jars to ensure they are airtight and store in a cool, dark place.

Here is a jam which costs next to nothing if you gather the fruit in the countryside, and deserves to be better known. It is delicious when diluted in water as a refreshing drink.

Prickly pear jam

INGREDIENTS

approx 6½lb / 3kg prickly pears

generous cup / 9fl oz / 250ml water

1 lemon or lime

4½ cups / 2½lb / 1kg sugar

METHOD

Wear heavy rubber gloves when peeling the prickly pears, slice off the ends first and remove the remaining skin. Place in a copper preserving pan with the water and a few pieces of lemon or lime peel.

Bring to the boil, then cook slowly for 5 minutes while stirring.

Remove from the heat and push through a very fine mesh sieve (to make a purée the consistency of clear honey).

Return the purée to the pan, add the sugar and return to a gentle boil, stirring and skimming every so often.

When the jam has reached setting point, turn off the heat and stir in the lemon or lime juice.

Ladle into jars which should be tightly sealed and stored in a cool, dark place.

The colour of this jam varies according to the variety of prickly pears used.

Sardinian, Sicilian, Moroccan and other Arab sweetmeats and desserts make use of this jam. In the United States the best fruit come from Opuntia magacantha *and are large and rose coloured. In Europe, the whitish or yellowish ones are best.*

Mint and apple jam

INGREDIENTS

¼lb / 100g (or more) young, tender peppermint leaves

2¼lb / 1kg, peeled, chopped apples

3 cups / 1½lb / 700g preserving sugar

2 lemons

METHOD

Drop the peeled, chopped apples into plenty of cold water acidulated with the juice of one lemon as you work, to prevent them turning brown. When they are all ready, drain and place in a preserving pan with the grated rind of one lemon, the very finely chopped mint leaves and a generous pinch of sugar.

Bring to a gentle boil, stirring and skimming, and cook until the apples are done. Remove from the heat and push through a fine sieve. Return this green purée to the pan, add the sugar and juice of the remaining lemon and bring back to the boil. Continue simmering, stirring and removing any scum, until the jam has reached setting point.

Remove from the heat and pour the hot jam into warmed jars, making sure they are hermetically sealed. Put away in a cool, dark storeroom.

A wonderfully refreshing jam for summertime; it can be diluted with water and chilled for a cool drink. It is also good with roast lamb.

Preserves and jams made with vegetables

Here is your chance to make
some very unusual preserves,
using such unlikely ingredients as carrots, pumpkin,
tomatoes and other garden produce:
bottled sunshine and vitamins for yourself
or for children during the long winter months.

Green tomato jam

Beet/beetroot preserve

INGREDIENTS

5½lb / 2½kg young, tender beets/beetroots
4½ cups / 2¼lb / 1kg sugar
1 lemon
1 orange
2-3 drops vanilla extract/essence

METHOD

Wash the beetroots well in cold water, chop off their leaves, leaving about ½in / 1cm of stalk, and add to a large saucepan full of boiling water; add a few pieces of lemon and orange peel (no pith), cover and boil for about 1½ hours.

When the beetroots are very tender, turn off the heat and leave to cool in the cooking water, then peel and dice or slice thinly.

Transfer the beetroots to a preserving pan. Add the sugar, vanilla, orange and lemon juice and stir. Leave to stand for an hour and then heat slowly to a gentle boil while stirring.

When the preserve has thickened sufficiently and has reached setting point, take off the heat and pour straight into the warmed jars, sealing without delay. Store the air-tight jars in a cool, dark place.

Only young beetroots should be used for this preserve – otherwise they will have developed woody, tough sections and fibrous parts.

Eggplant/aubergine preserve

INGREDIENTS

6½lb / 3kg firm, ripe eggplants/aubergines, trimmed, washed and peeled
4½lb / 2kg sugar
2 apples (peeled and cored)
2 lemons

METHOD

Dice the prepared eggplants/aubergines and apples and place in the preserving pan; sprinkle with the juice of both lemons and the grated rind of only one. Stir in the sugar. Bring slowly to the boil while stirring and removing any scum with a wooden spoon.

Simmer gently until the eggplants/aubergines are soft and pulpy; from this point onwards they will stick and burn very easily. When the preserve has reached the correct consistency, remove from the heat and pour into warmed jars. Make sure the lids are airtight. Keep in a cool, dark place.

This recipe originally called for the eggplant variety which gave the vegetable its name – white and looking just like an egg. Nowadays only those with gardens are likely to find them easy to come by; the purple ones will do very well. Serve as a relish with roast goose, duck or turkey.

Sweet (bell) pepper jam

INGREDIENTS

9lb / 4kg ripe, plump and firm peppers

4½lb / 2kg sugar

1 lemon

small piece vanilla pod

small piece cinnamon bark

METHOD

Rinse, dry and quarter the peppers; remove stalk, pith and seeds. Chop into small pieces; this should yield about 6½lb / 3kg of prepared, chopped flesh. Place in a bowl with the sugar, the grated peel, the juice of the lemon and the vanilla and cinnamon. Stir and leave to stand for 1 hour (remove vanilla and cinnamon after ½ hour, or stir in a drop of vanilla essence and a pinch of ground cinnamon). Transfer to a preserving pan and cook very gently, stirring and skimming.

When the mixture has just reached boiling point, cook a little faster until the mixture is thick enough when tested.

Remove from the heat, transfer to jars while hot, and seal tightly. Storage should be cool and dark.

You can either mix the yellow and red peppers for multi-coloured jam, or make a batch of red and a batch of yellow jam. It is particularly good when served with roast game, duck or turkey.

Rhubarb jam

INGREDIENTS

5½lb / 2½kg pale pink or white tender rhubarb

6½ cups / 3¼lb / 1½kg sugar

2 lemons

METHOD

Wash the young rhubarb stems well after trimming, and plunge into a basinful of cold water acidulated with the juice of 1 lemon. Cut the stems into lengths of about ½in / 1cm, discarding any tough or stringy pieces.

Place in a large bowl; sprinkle with the juice of the remaining lemon and stir in the sugar. Leave to stand for 12 hours. The rhubarb will release plenty of juice: this should be poured into the preserving pan and boiled until reduced to just under half its original volume. Add the rhubarb pieces and cook until mushy, stirring and removing scum when this forms. When the mixture thickens and clings to the ladle or metal spoon used for skimming, remove from the heat; transfer the hot jam into jars and seal tightly at once. Store in a dry, dark place.

This jam is an excellent filling for tarts, flans and cakes. Use the year's second, autumn crop, as it has far more flavour.

Pumpkin jam

INGREDIENTS

approx 3¼lb / 1½kg pumpkin (ripe and sound)
2 cups / 1lb / 500g sugar
1 vanilla pod
1 lemon (peel only)
¼ cup / 2fl oz / 50ml brandy
a sufficient quantity of water

METHOD

Peel the pumpkin, cut the flesh into pieces and steam until only just tender; dice and weigh.

Weigh out sugar to match the cooked pumpkin weight; place sugar in a preserving pan, add enough water to just cover; add the vanilla pod and boil gently until it forms a thick syrup. Wash and dry the lemon; grate all the peel and add to the sugar syrup together with the pumpkin. Cook over a moderate heat, mixing frequently, for 25 minutes. Add the brandy, remove the vanilla pod and cook for a furthe 5 minutes. To test if it is set, put one drop of jam on to a tilted plate: it should run down the surface very slowly. Transfer to jars and allow to cool before storing in a dry, dark place.

If hermetic-seal (Mason or Kilner type) jars are not used, cover each jar with Saran wrap/clingfilm and secure with string or rubber bands; puncture the wrap with tiny holes; the surface of the jam will harden into a protective covering, while letting the jam breathe.

Carrot jam

INGREDIENTS

2¼lb / 1kg carrots
2¼lb / 1kg sugar
4 lemons

METHOD

Scrub or scrape the carrots; wash, cut into thin discs and boil in just enough water to cover; when tender, drain, reserving a scant cup / 7fl oz / 200ml of the water; stir the sugar into the water and set aside.

Purée the carrots in a food mill or food processor, transfer to a saucepan and mix in the sweetened hot cooking liquid. Cook over a low heat, stirring continuously with a wooden spoon, until the jam thickens so that it can only just be shaken off the spoon. Remove from the heat; allow to cool before stirring in the juice and finely grated peel of the lemons.

Transfer to jars, seal tightly and keep in a cool, dark place.

Try this jam spread on buttered slices of bread, for breakfast or for a snack.

Green tomato jam

INGREDIENTS

6½lb / 3kg green tomatoes
4lb / 1.8kg sugar
2 lemons
¼ cup / 2fl oz / 50ml brandy

METHOD *(see illustrated instructions on page 188)*

Wash the tomatoes in cold water, cut in half, squeeze out the seeds and chop roughly, placing the flesh in a bowl. Add the sugar, grated rind of one lemon, the strained juice of both lemons and stir well. Pour into a preserving pan and boil for 5 minutes, stirring and removing any scum as necessary.

When the tomatoes are fairly mushy and tender, remove from the heat, push through a sieve and return the purée to the pan. Simmer until it looks thick and glossy.

Test a drop of the jam using the normal method: when the plate is tipped up slightly it should travel down it very slowly.

Remove from the heat and stir in the brandy. Ladle the hot jam into warmed jars and seal tightly. Dry, dark storage will help the jam keep well.

Slightly riper tomatoes, which are still hard, can also be used for this recipe.

Tomato jam

INGREDIENTS

6½lb / 3kg firm ripe red tomatoes
4lb / 1.8kg sugar
2 lemons
1 cup / 8fl oz / 225ml spirit or liqueur of your choice (rum, brandy, etc.)

METHOD

Wash the tomatoes in plenty of cold water, cut in half and squeeze out the seeds and excess juice. Put the flesh in a preserving pan and add the juice of both lemons with the grated rind of one.

Bring to the boil; you will only need to stir the tomatoes occasionally but remove any scum at frequent intervals. Boil for 5 minutes before removing from the heat and pushing through a fine sieve. Pour the purée back into the pan and add the sugar.

Continue cooking while stirring and skimming until the mixture reaches the consistency of a preserve or jam and looks thick, syrupy and bright red. Stir in the spirit or liqueur.

Remove from the heat and pour into jars while still hot, sealing tightly. Store in a dry, dark place.

This makes a good filling for tarts and small, individual strudels.

Jellies made with wild and garden produce

Jewel-coloured jars of translucent jelly
are the reward of the cook who,
with patience and skill,
can produce an appetizing
and decorative finishing touch for flans,
tarts and fruit confectionery.

Apricot jelly

Apricot jelly

INGREDIENTS

4½lb / 2kg sound, ripe apricots
4½lb / 2kg preserving sugar
2 lemons

METHOD

Wash the apricots well and dry on paper towels. Cut in half, removing the pits/stones. Place in a large preserving pan and add enough water to cover them by ¼in / ½cm. Add the grated rind of one lemon. Cover and bring to a gentle boil, removing scum when necessary.

When the apricots are very tender and mushy, remove from the heat and push through a fine hair sieve or put into a jelly bag to strain while still hot.

Collect the juice in a bowl and stir in the sugar and the juice of both lemons. Return to the pan and bring back to a slow boil, skimming at intervals. When the jelly has thickened to a consistency nearly as thick as honey, remove the pan from the heat.

Pour the hot jelly immediately into warmed jars. Seal tightly and keep in a cool, dark place.

This jelly is invaluable for glazing puff pastry fruit tarts or sponge fruit flans and for topping ice-cream sundaes.

Morello cherry jelly

INGREDIENTS

4½lb / 2kg sound ripe pitted/stoned cherries
1lb / 500g redcurrants
4½lb / 2kg preserving sugar
1 lemon
1 quart / 1¾ pints / 1 litre water

METHOD

Wash the Morello cherries and pit/stone before weighing and placing in a preserving pan.

Add the redcurrants (their stalks removed), water and the lemon peel (pared thinly, leaving behind all the bitter white pith).

Bring to a slow boil and cook for 10 minutes, skimming and stirring every now and then with a wooden spoon.

When it is time to turn off the heat, put the fruit into a jelly bag and hang up to strain. If clarity is not important, squeeze the bag well when nearly all the juice has dripped into the bowl below. Pour the juice into the pan; add the sugar and lemon juice. Bring to the boil, skimming frequently, and cook until a deep blood red. Remove from the heat, pour into prepared jars and seal tightly. Keep cool and away from light.

Use acid cherries for this jelly: Morello, Montmorency or sharp, wild cherries.

Orange jelly

INGREDIENTS

5 juicy oranges
4 dessert apples (Reinette or Russet type)
3 cups / 1¼lb / 600g sugar
3¼ cups / 1¼ pints / 750ml water

METHOD

Remove and discard the peel and pith from two of the oranges. Pare off all the peel from the other three oranges, leaving behind all the white pith, and put the parings to one side. Then peel off the pith from these oranges.

Chop the flesh coarsely, wasting none of the juice which, with the flesh, should weigh 1lb / 500g.

Peel and chop the apples (this should yield about 1lb / 500g). Place the apples, oranges and parings in a preserving pan with the water. Bring to the boil and then simmer gently until the apples are very tender (their pectin will set the jelly). Either push through a fine plastic or stainless steel sieve or strain in a jelly bag.

Sieving will yield about 2¼lb / 1kg purée; straining gives a far smaller volume of liquid but the jelly will have great clarity. Mix in the sugar and bring to the boil in the pan for about 20 minutes.

When the gelatin has reached setting point (this happens suddenly, so test frequently), remove from the heat and pour straight into jars. Make sure they are airtight and store in a dry, dark place.

Set the sieved, purée version in shallow trays; cut into squares, roll in superfine/caster sugar for delicious and wholesome treats for children.

Persimmon jelly

INGREDIENTS

5½lb / 2½kg very ripe persimmons
4½ cups / 2¼lb / 1kg preserving sugar
1 lemon
1 cup / 8fl oz / 225ml water

METHOD

If you use Sharon fruit, they are ripe when still fairly firm. Wash, remove the stem and calyx, and spoon out all the flesh into a non-metallic sieve. Weigh the resulting purée (it should yield about 2¼lb / 1kg).

Make a sugar syrup, boiling the sugar, water and thinly pared lemon peel in a preserving pan, stirring with a wooden spoon, until it reaches the large-thread stage, that is 219°F / 104°C or 38° Baumé (see page 99).

Remove and discard the lemon peel and stir in the persimmon purée and lemon juice.

Continue cooking over a low heat until the jelly reaches setting point. Remove from the heat and pour the hot jelly into jars. Store under dry, dark conditions.

Persimmons must look overripe: if used before, they will be bitter and leave an unpleasant coating sensation in the mouth.

Raspberry jelly

INGREDIENTS

4½lb / 2kg ripe raspberries
10½ cups / 5¼lb / 2.4kg preserving sugar
1 lemon
2 cups / 18fl oz / 500 ml water

METHOD

Crush the washed, drained raspberries, squeezing them by hand, and place in a large bowl.

Stir in the water, the juice and the thinly pared peel of the lemon and leave to stand for 2 hours.

Transfer to a preserving pan and boil gently for about 10 minutes, skimming. Remove from the heat and push through a fine non-metallic sieve, or strain through a jelly bag, squeezing tightly.

Return the liquid to the pan and add the sugar. Bring to the boil once more and cook gently while stirring and skimming until the jelly reaches setting point.

Turn off the heat immediately once the correct consistency has been reached and pour straightaway into warmed jars, making sure the lids are airtight. Keep in a cool, dark place.

Pick your raspberries once the early sun of a midsummer morning has dispersed the dew or in the early evening, never in the hotter parts of the day.

Mandarin jelly

INGREDIENTS

10 mandarin oranges
3¼lb / 1½kg dessert apples (Russet or Reinette type) or quinces
6½ cups / 3¼lb / 1½kg preserving sugar
1 lemon
3¼ cups / 1¼ pints / 750ml water

METHOD

Peel but do not core the apples and cook them in 2¼ cups / 18fl oz / 550ml water, removing any scum. When they are mushy, remove from the heat and strain off the juice through a fine non-metallic sieve (or strain in a jelly bag). Squeeze the juice of the mandarins and the lemon into a bowl and stir in the thinly pared peel (no pith) of the lemon and 4-5 mandarins.

Make a sugar syrup by boiling the sugar gently with a scant cup / 7fl oz / 200ml water, until it is as thick as honey but still clear and uncoloured (do not stir); it will take about 5 minutes to thicken. Remove from the heat and carefully add the apple juice and mandarin juice and peels. Boil for 1 or 2 minutes; turn off the heat, leave to stand for 15 minutes and then strain, discarding the peels.

Return to the heat and simmer, skimming and stirring, until it reaches setting point. Pour into prepared jars, seal well and keep in a dry, dark place.

Other citrus-mandarin crossed fruits can be made into jellies following this recipe; as an exquisite luxury, try kumquats.

Apricot tarts covered with Apricot jelly

Blackberry (bramble) jelly

INGREDIENTS

- *$4\frac{1}{2}$lb / 2kg sound, ripe blackberries*
- *1lb / 500g peeled and sliced apples*
- *$6\frac{1}{2}$ cups / 3lb 5oz / $1\frac{1}{2}$kg preserving sugar*
- *2 lemons*
- *1 vanilla pod*

METHOD

Place the washed, drained blackberries in a preserving pan. Add the apples, the peel and juice of 1 lemon and bring to the boil over a high heat; add the vanilla and keep stirring and skimming.

Allow to boil for 8-10 minutes, crushing the blackberries and apples as they cook so that they turn mushy. When the boiling time is up, remove from the heat and strain in a jelly bag, twisting to extract all the juice if the clarity of the jelly is not important. Return the juice to the pan, and stir in the sugar and the juice of the remaining lemon.

Bring to the boil again and then simmer gently, stirring and removing any scum. Cook for 15-20 minutes, or until the jelly reaches setting point.

Pour the hot jelly into prepared jars and leave to cool completely before sealing. Keep in a cool, dark cupboard or cellar.

Include a few slightly underripe blackberries; as well as improving the set, these red berries will add a pleasant hint of acidity to the jelly.

Grapefruit jelly

INGREDIENTS

- *5 very juicy, ripe grapefruit*
- *4 dessert apples (Reinette or Russet type)*
- *$4\frac{1}{2}$ cups / $2\frac{1}{4}$lb / 1kg preserving sugar*
- *2 cups / 18fl oz / 500ml water*

METHOD

Peel the grapefruit, removing all the pith, and chop the flesh coarsely, collecting the juice (together these should weigh about 1lb / 500g). Peel and chop the apples (again, net weight should be 1lb / 500g).

Place the grapefruit and apples in a preserving pan with the water. Bring to the boil and then cook over a low heat until the apples are cooked through. Push through a fine, non-metallic sieve (alternatively, strain in a jelly bag, in which case all the apple flesh and some of the grapefruit will be left behind, yielding much less jelly, but what there is will be very clear). Add the sugar to the liquid (which should weigh about $2\frac{1}{4}$lb / 1kg) and return to the boil for 10-15 minutes.

When the jelly has reached the correct consistency (which it does quite suddenly, so keep testing), remove from the heat and pour straight into warmed jars; seal tightly and put away in a cool, dry place.

Grapefruit are low in calories, only about 24-25 per $3\frac{1}{3}$ oz / 100g, because of their low sugar content.

Sunshine blackcurrant jelly

INGREDIENTS

6½lb / 3kg blackcurrants (taken off stalks)
7lb / 3.2kg preserving sugar
2 lemons

METHOD

Wash and drain the blackcurrants before using a fork to remove their stalks; spread out in a single layer to dry in the sun for about 1 hour. Push through a fine, non-metallic sieve, pressing hard with your hands or a large wooden spoon, letting the juice drop into a large non-metallic bowl. Add the sugar, the juice of both lemons and a few pieces of thinly pared peel (these last will be discarded later).

Mix with a wooden spoon and leave to stand for 2 hours, stirring to ensure the sugar dissolves totally. Remove the lemon peel and pour into absolutely clean glass jam jars; stand these in hot sunlight, with a piece of fine cheesecloth / muslin covering each jar to protect from wasps. The jars must stand in the sun for 3 days or thereabouts, to clock up a total of 15-20 hours' exposure to sunlight. When they have done so, seal tightly in the usual way and keep cool and dark.

This jelly is a good one to try during a spell of very hot weather. Orange juice or mandarin juice makes a pleasant addition to the jelly.

Sorb apple jelly

INGREDIENTS

3½lb / 1.6kg sorb apples
4 dessert apples (Reinette or Russet type)
1lb / 500g preserving sugar for each 2 cups / 18fl oz / 500ml liquid

METHOD

For jelly making, sorbs should be picked when they appear ripe, coloured yellow and red, just before they are ready to fall from the tree (for eating they must fall and be left to "blet" - they are only palatable raw when they appear brown and rotten!). Remove the stalks, wash and bring to a gentle boil in the preserving pan with the chopped cored apples and enough water to cover. When the fruit is tender, remove from the heat, crush the fruit roughly and place in a jelly bag; if you twist it gently you will get all the juice out but the jelly will not be so clear.

Pour the thick juice into an earthenware fireproof cooking pot and simmer gently for about 20 minutes; then weigh the juice and add sugar as shown in ingredients. Stir well, bring back to the boil and simmer slowly until the jelly reaches setting point, skimming frequently.

Allow to cool and thicken; transfer to jars and keep in a cool, dark place.

Soak the sorb apples in several changes of cold water for 2 days before using them. This jelly goes very well with furred or feathered game. It is best to wait a year for the full flavour to develop before opening the jars!

Plum jelly

INGREDIENTS

6½lb / 3kg ripe yellow plums
4½lb / 2kg preserving sugar
1 lemon

METHOD

Rinse the plums briefly under cold water, drain and spread out to dry on cloths or paper towels.

Push the plum flesh through a fine, non-metallic sieve, leaving the pits/stones and skins behind; this will yield about 4½lb / 2kg of purée.

Stir in the lemon juice and grated rind and the sugar, and transfer the purée to a preserving pan. Bring to a gentle boil, stirring frequently and skimming; cook until the jelly reaches setting point. Remove from the heat and pour into the jars while still hot, placing airtight lids on the jars immediately. Store in a dry, dark place.

Golden Drop is the best variety of plum to use for jelly; Pershore or Mirabelles would do as well. This jelly can be used to make hot or cold drinks and milk shakes, to glaze tarts and fruit flans, and is an excellent base for fools or cold soufflés.

Gooseberry jelly

INGREDIENTS

4½lb / 2kg gooseberries
equivalent quantity of preserving sugar to net weight of purée (see method)
3/2 tablespoons white wine (or cider) vinegar
1 quart / 1¾ pints / 1 litre water
3-4 mint leaves

METHOD

Remove the stalks from the gooseberries, wash, and drain; place in a preserving pan with the white wine vinegar and water, and cook slowly until the gooseberries are tender and their skins have split. Strain in a non-metallic sieve or jelly bag. Weigh the juice and add an equal weight of sugar (or allow 1lb / 450g sugar to each US 1¼ pints / UK 1pint / 550ml liquid). Return to the pan and bring to a gentle boil again with the mint leaves. Test the jelly at intervals to see whether it has reached setting point (see pages 11-12).

Discard the mint leaves and allow to cool before potting; keep in a dry, dark place.

Gooseberry jelly complements roast lamb and spit-roasted game birds, such as quail, to perfection.

Wine jelly

INGREDIENTS

2¼lb / 1kg dessert apples (Reinette or Russet type) or quinces, chopped

1½ quarts / 2 pints 13fl oz / 1½ litres good, pure red wine

4½lb / 2kg preserving sugar

2 lemons

METHOD

Place the peeled, chopped apples (do not core) in a preserving pan with 1 quart / 1¾ pints / 1 litre wine and the juice and peel of 1 lemon. Cook until the apples are mushy (quinces will take longer, so add a generous cup / 9fl oz / 250ml water as well), strain through a non-metallic fine sieve or jelly bag, squeezing well to extract all the juice. This should yield about 3¼lb / 1½kg of rather cloudy thick juice. Stir in the remaining wine, the sugar and the juice of the other lemon.

Return to the heat and simmer, removing any scum; the juice will gradually clear and will slowly thicken like any other jelly (taking about 30-35 minutes).

Remove from the heat and pour the hot jelly into jars, sealing tightly. See that your storage is cool and dark.

If quinces are used, the flavour will be more pronounced with a pleasant note of acidity.

Black Forest jelly

INGREDIENTS

2¼lb / 1kg blackcurrants (or blueberries/bilberries)

2¼lb / 1kg raspberries

approx ¾lb / 350g wild or Alpine strawberries

4lb / 1.8kg preserving sugar

1 lemon

METHOD

Crush the blackcurrants and raspberries well, extracting all the juice – which should be fairly thick and weigh 3¼lb / 1½kg. Stir in the sugar, lemon juice and peel (to be removed after cooking). Transfer to a preserving pan and bring very slowly to a gentle simmer, skimming when necessary. When the mixture starts to thicken, remove the peel, stir almost continuously and skim from time to time.

When the jelly has almost reached setting point, tip in the strawberries and continue cooking gently, mixing the strawberries into the jelly.

Be careful not to overcook: the pan should be taken off the heat each time you test for setting, otherwise the colour, taste and set will suffer and the jelly may crystallize.

Once the strawberries drop to the bottom of the pan when you stop stirring, and setting point is reached, pour into jars and seal at once while still hot. Keep in a cool, dark place.

Use the fruit the same day it has been picked for successful jelly and jam.

Fruit preserved in syrup

A marvellous, ready-to-serve dessert:
sweet, delicate and versatile;
serve on its own or with vanilla ice-cream,
topped with swirls of whipped cream,
with egg custard, or even with your
favourite spirit or liqueur.
A treat to transform any meal.

Pineapple rings in syrup
Pineapple jam

Apricots in syrup

INGREDIENTS

7lb / 3.2kg perfectly sound, firm ripe apricots
¾lb / 350g preserving sugar
1 lemon (peel only)
1 quart / 1¾ pints / 1 litre water

METHOD

Rinse the apricots briefly but thoroughly under the cold tap; dry well with a clean cloth; ideally, spread them out to dry for ½-1 hour.

Make a sugar syrup by mixing the sugar, water and a small piece of lemon peel and then boiling gently for 2-3 minutes; leave to cool.

Use a small, sharp knife to cut the apricots in half; discard the pits/stones. Pack the apricots, rounded side upwards, into Kilner or similar preserving jars. Seal the jars and sterilize for 20-25 minutes (method on page 119 or follow directions given with the various types of patent jars).

Store in a dry, dark place, after checking to see that the seal is perfectly airtight. Check the seal after 24 hours: if the clamps or screw bands are removed you should be able to pick the jar up holding its lid (above the seal). If the seal has failed, re-process.

Any sign of cloudiness means the apricots must be eaten at once.

Pineapple rings in syrup

INGREDIENTS

5 or 6 fresh, firm pineapples
4½ cups / 2¼lb / 1kg sugar
1 lemon
approx 1½ quarts / 2 pints 13fl oz / 1½ litres water
¼ cup / 2fl oz / 50ml maraschino or kirsch

METHOD

Cut off both ends of each pineapple and remove all the skin. Slice into rings ¼-½in / ½-1cm thick; use an apple corer to remove the tough centre of each slice.

Place in a shallow dish and sprinkle with the juice of the lemon.

Make a sugar syrup by boiling the water with the sugar for 5 minutes; there is no need to stir.

Pack the pineapple rings into the bottling jars. Add a small piece of lemon peel (no pith) and a few drops of maraschino or kirsch to each before pouring in the hot sugar syrup and sealing. Sterilize for 30-35 minutes (see page 119). Check the seal (see preceding recipe). Keep in a cool, dark place.

An ideal dessert when served with lemon ice-cream in individual sundae dishes.

Pineapple rings in syrup

Oranges in syrup

INGREDIENTS

15 large, juicy oranges
4½ cups / 2¼lb / 1kg sugar
¼ cup / 2fl oz / 50ml kirsch
2¼ quarts / 4 pints / 2¼ litres water

METHOD

Pare off and reserve the peel from two oranges, leaving behind all the pith. Peel all the other oranges, working over a bowl. Use a small very sharp knife to cut away rind and pith, down to the quick, exposing the juicy flesh; slip the blade inside the membranes separating the segments and detach them, placing them in the bowl.

Pack into the jars as tightly and neatly as possible, adding the juice. Make a sugar syrup by boiling the sugar, water and the two orange peels for 5 minutes; leave to cool slightly. Discard the peel, add the kirsch and pour the warm syrup into the jars so that the orange segments are covered.

Seal the jars and sterilize for 20-25 minutes (see page 119). Store under cool, dark conditions.

Wait at least a month before tasting these oranges; serve them just as they are or with a fruit purée sauce.

Cherries in syrup

INGREDIENTS

6½lb / 3kg sound, firm, ripe cherries (wild, Morello or Red Acid varieties)
1lb / 450-500g sugar
1 quart / 1¾ pints / 1 litre water
1 lemon
a few drops maraschino essence or liqueur (optional)

METHOD

Place the cherries in a sink full of cold water and swish around gently, taking care not to bruise them. Drain, remove the stalks and spread the cherries out to dry. Pack into jars. Make a sugar syrup by boiling the water with the sugar and a few pieces of lemon peel. When it has cooked for 3-4 minutes, leave to cool.

Pour the cold sugar syrup into the jars to come three-quarters of the way up the jar (i.e., not covering the top third of the cherries).

For a very definite flavour, add a few drops of maraschino essence or, as this can sometimes only be found in very specialized grocers, a little liqueur or cherry brandy.

Make sure the jars are airtight when sealed and sterilize for 20-30 minutes (see method on page 119).

Keep in a cool, dark place.

Serve in individual glass sundae dishes, topped with whipped cream, or add to milk shakes or ice-cream sodas for refreshing summer drinks.

Cornelian cherries (cornels) in syrup

INGREDIENTS

4½lb / 2kg perfectly sound, ripe cornels
1 lemon
3½ cups / 1¾lb / 800g sugar
1 quart / 1¾ pints / 1 litre water

METHOD

Remove the stalks from the fruit carefully so as not to tear the skin or flesh. Rinse briefly in cold water and spread out on a clean cloth to dry.

Pack into jars (there is no need to pit/stone). Boil the sugar and water together for 2 minutes with a piece or two of lemon peel.

Remove the syrup from the heat and stir in the juice of the lemon. Pour into the jars, so that the syrup comes three-quarters of the way up each jarful of cornels. Seal tightly and sterilize for 20-30 minutes (see method on page 119). Test for seal 24 hours afterwards. Keep in a dry, dark place.

Cornels look rather like very beautiful red olives and have a somewhat sour taste even when sweetened. Use these as a most attractive edible garnish for roast meats.

Strawberries in syrup

INGREDIENTS

4½lb / 2kg sound, barely ripe wild or Alpine strawberries, all the same size (or cultivated strawberries)
1lb / 500g sugar
1 quart / 1¾ pints / 1 litre water
1 lemon (peel only)
approx ¼ cup / 2fl oz / 50ml brandy or liqueur

METHOD

Do not wash the strawberries unless they are gritty or muddy, when they should be rinsed for a second or two under cold water; dry well on paper towels or spread out in the sun, turning frequently, for 1 hour. Pack the strawberries into small preserving jars.

Make the sugar syrup, boiling the sugar and water for 3-5 minutes. Pour over the strawberries in the jars while still boiling hot, to come three-quarters of the way up the jars. Place a piece of lemon peel in each jar.

Prolonged sterilization is to be avoided with such delicate fruits as strawberries which turn mushy when cooked, so pour about 1 teaspoon of warmed brandy inside the lid of each jar, set light to it and carefully invert it over the jar and seal. The alcohol will continue to burn until it has used up all the oxygen inside the jar.

Sterilize the sealed jars for about 5 minutes and test the lids to make sure the seal is perfect (see pages 119-120). Keep the strawberries dry and dark.

These make a good filling, either on their own or with other fruit, for pies and tarts; very useful for enhancing fruit salads and all sorts of desserts.

Oranges in syrup

Mixed fruit in aquavit

INGREDIENTS

11lb / 5kg sound, ripe raspberries, cherries, blueberries/bilberries, apricots, pears, plums and peaches	
approx 4 quarts / 7 pints / 4 litres aquavit, brandy or marc	
4½lb / 2kg sugar	
1¼ cups / ½ pint / 300ml water	

METHOD

Avoid washing the fruit if possible, wiping instead with a slightly damp cloth and drying gently. If it must be washed, handle as little as possible and dry completely.

Pit/stone the cherries and plums. Cut the apricots and peaches in half and remove the pits/stones. Cut the pears into quarters and, working quickly so that the pears will not have time to discolour, pack the fruit mixture into jars in layers or like a fruit salad. Pour in enough aquavit or brandy to cover and place the lids on the jars; clamp or screw shut and leave to stand for 1 week in a dry, dark place.

When the week is up, make a sugar syrup by bringing the sugar and water to the boil (do not stir). Once it has boiled, remove from the heat (it must not colour at all) and leave to cool. Pour the cold syrup into the jars. Seal tightly and keep in a dark, dry place.

These preserved fruits can be used for decorative effect on desserts or eaten in small quantities at the end of a meal, to round if off. The juice makes a marvellous liqueur.

Raspberries in syrup

INGREDIENTS

4½lb / 2kg slightly underripe, sound raspberries	
2½ cups / 1¼lb / 600g sugar	
1 lemon	
1 quart / 1¾ pints / 1 litre water	

METHOD

Pick the raspberries once the dew has evaporated; they should be slightly underripe, deep pink rather than red. Always bottle them the same day, the sooner the better.

Place the dry raspberries in jars. Boil the sugar, water and lemon peel for 2-3 minutes. Remove from the heat, stir in the lemon juice and pour into the jars while still hot, so that the syrup comes three-quarters of the way up the jars.

Seal the jars tightly and sterilize for 10 minutes (see page 119 or follow instructions given with patent bottling jars); have the water at a gentle simmer rather than a brisk boil, as raspberries are very delicate.

Test to ensure that the seal is effective, and keep in a dry, dark place.

Never pick raspberries when it is hot and preferably not in full sunlight. The slightly underripe raspberries will break up less easily if picked with care; do not pile them up on top of each other and avoid washing them if possible.

Fruit salad in syrup

INGREDIENTS

8¾lb / 4kg (peeled weight) apples, pears, peaches, apricots, gooseberries, cherries, pineapple
1 lemon
2 quarts / 3½ pints / 2 litres water
4½ cups / 2¼lb / 1kg sugar

METHOD

Prepare and peel all the fruit and cut into pieces (about the size of the halved cherries), sprinkling the apples and pears with lemon juice as they are prepared.

Mix all the fruit gently but thoroughly and place in the jars.

Make a sugar syrup: boil the water with the sugar for 2 minutes. Remove from the heat and pour while hot into the jars.

Seal and sterilize for 20 minutes (see page 119). Put away in a cool, dark store cupboard or cellar.

A boon when it comes to filling pastry cases which have been baked "blind" (baked with greaseproof paper and white beans to hold their shape when cooked without a filling). A layer of crème patissière can be spread over the case, to be topped by the fruit. You can vary the fruits according to the season.

Mandarins in syrup

INGREDIENTS

3¼lb / 1½kg mandarins
1lb / 500g sugar
scant cup / 7fl oz / 200ml water
1 lemon (peel only)

METHOD

Pick out perfectly sound mandarins, open one in advance and check on the flesh, which should be firm and juicy.

Peel, separate the segments and pull the little fibres from the sharp edge and any pith from the outside of the segments, without tearing the membrane at all; there will be about 2¼lb / 1kg of segments. Pack them into jars as you work. Tap the base of each jar on an oven glove or thick cloth covering the table to make them settle and put a few pieces of lemon peel in each jar.

Prepare the sugar syrup by mixing the sugar and water, heating until it boils, and the moment the sugar has dissolved, pour into the jars, covering the mandarins. Seal well, sterilize for 10-15 minutes (see page 119) and place in cool, dark storage after testing the seal.

For a less sugary taste, make the sugar syrup with 1⅓ cups / 10½oz / 300g sugar and generous 1½ cups / 14fl oz / 400ml water; mix, boil until dissolved and leave to cool. Pour the cold syrup into the jars and seal. Sterilize for about 10 minutes.

Add the mandarins and their syrup to fruit salads; use the segments in ice-cream sundaes or to fill cooked open flan or tart cases.

Sweet chestnuts in syrup

INGREDIENTS

5½lb / 2½kg sound, sweet (Spanish) chestnuts
3½ cups / 1¾lb / 800g sugar
1 lemon
1 orange
1 quart / 1¾ pints / 1 litre water
5-6 fennel seeds (or a piece of fennel stalk)
few small pieces vanilla pod

METHOD

Add the chestnuts, unskinned, to a large pan of cold water with a piece of orange peel and the fennel seeds (or stalk). Boil until nearly cooked inside (test one). Meanwhile, make a sugar syrup, boiling the sugar, water and lemon juice for 2-3 minutes; remove from the heat and leave to cool.

Take the chestnuts off the heat when they are almost done and leave to cool in the liquid until they are just cool enough to handle; remove both the hard outer and thin inner skins very carefully (this will take time and patience), placing them in the jars as you progress. Keep them as intact as possible, but it does not matter if a few broken ones are included. Place a piece of lemon peel and a piece of vanilla pod about the size of a match head in each jar.

Cover the chestnuts with the syrup, seal tightly and sterilize for 20 minutes (see page 119). Keep in a cool dark place.

These chestnuts can decorate cakes or desserts or provide a mouth-watering dessert – marrons with crème chantilly or Mont Blanc.

Melons in their own syrup

INGREDIENTS

6½lb / 3kg full-flavoured, aromatic melons (Charentais or Cantaloupe)
4lb / 1.8kg sugar
2 lemons

METHOD

Scrub the outside of the melons with a stiff brush under cold running water.

Cut each one horizontally in half; spoon out the seeds and filaments. Slice into wedges and then peel each wedge with a very sharp knife (to yield about 4½lb / 2kg net weight). Cut into small, thin pieces about ¼in / ½cm wide. Soak up all the excess moisture with paper towels.

Arrange the melon pieces in jars, alternating layers of sugar and melon; sprinkle each layer with a few drops of lemon juice.

Seal tightly and sterilize for 15-20 minutes (see page 119). Keep in dry, dark storage.

The pieces of melon and the syrup which they produce can add the finishing touch to a fruit salad or add an extra something to vanilla or lemon ice-cream desserts.

Melon in syrup
Melon jam

Melons in syrup

INGREDIENTS

- *6½lb / 3kg melons*
- *3½ cups / 1¾lb / 800g sugar*
- *2 lemons*
- *4 quarts / 7 pints / 4 litres water*
- *port according to taste*

METHOD

Cut the melons in half and spoon out the seeds and fibres from the centre, and the very soft area of the central "well". Cut into fairly large slices or smaller pieces, removing the peel. This should yield about 4½lb / 2kg flesh.

Bring 3 quarts / 5¼ pints / 3 litres water to the boil with 1¼ cup / 10oz / 300g sugar and the juice of 1½ lemons.

As soon as it boils add the melon pieces, making sure they are covered by the syrup. Remove from the heat immediately and leave to stand for 5 minutes. Remove the melon pieces from the syrup with a slotted spoon.

Pack the well-drained melon into jars. Make a thicker syrup, bringing 1 quart / 1¾ pints / 1 litre of the thin syrup, the remaining sugar and a piece of lemon peel to the boil; as soon as it boils, pour over the melon, to come three-quarters of the way up the jars.

Seal while still hot and sterilize for 30 minutes (see page 119). Keep in a dry, dark place.

Choose very fragrant melons, full of flavour - Charentais, Cantaloupe or Cavaillac - which are not too ripe. Add a few drops of ruby port to each jar before sealing if wished.

Blueberries/bilberries in syrup

INGREDIENTS

- *4½lb / 2kg blueberries/bilberries*
- *1½lb / 700g sugar*
- *1 lemon*
- *1 quart / 1¾ pints / 1 litre water*

METHOD

Do not wash the blueberries/bilberries, but check them, removing any stalks, leaves, etc. Place them in jars with a piece of lemon peel in each.

Mix the water and sugar and boil for 2-4 minutes; remove from the heat and sprinkle in the lemon juice. Pour the hot syrup into the jars; its level inside the jars should come three-quarters of the way up the blueberries/bilberries. Seal tightly and sterilize for about 30 minutes (see page 119).

They should be stored in a dry, dark place.

When summer is long gone you will be able to make a delicious fruit fool or cold soufflé or, more simply, enjoy the berries with ice-cream or in a fruit salad.

Melons in syrup and Melon jam

Blackberries in syrup

INGREDIENTS

2¼lb / 1kg wild blackberries
1¾ cups / 14oz / 400g sugar
1¼ cups / 11fl oz / 300ml water
1 lemon

METHOD

If possible, avoid washing the blackberries. Place them in sterilized jars, pour a little lemon juice in each jar and add a piece of peel; as you fill the jars, tap their bases on a folded cloth on the table to make sure they settle well down in the jar.

Make the sugar syrup: add the sugar to the water and boil for 3 minutes. Remove from the heat and pour straight into the jars, to come three-quarters of the way up the blackberries. Seal tightly at once and sterilize for 10 minutes (see page 119) by lowering them into boiling water. Test the seal 24 hours afterwards and keep in a cool, dark place.

Gather blackberries from high up on the bushes, away from roadsides where they are liable to be dirty. Choose full, firm, ripe berries which are not damaged or dirty.

Peaches in syrup

INGREDIENTS

8¾lb / 4kg sound, firm clingstone (yellow) peaches of equal size
6 cups / 3lb 1oz / 1.4kg sugar
2½ quarts / 4 pints 8fl oz / 2½ litres water
2 lemons

METHOD

Place a large preserving pan of water to heat with the juice of both lemons and a few pieces of peel. When the water reaches a very gentle boil, lower the peaches into it a few at a time, poaching them for ½-1 minute, depending on how ripe they are.

Drain each batch and immerse immediately in plenty of cold (or iced) water, using a large colander for both operations. Quickly peel the blanched peaches; they should not be left in the water for any length of time. Dry each one as soon as it is peeled with a clean cloth or paper towels. Halve and pit/stone them; spread out, rounded side uppermost, to dry completely in the sun (or in a warm place) for 1 hour.

Bring the sugar and water to the boil, remove from the heat at once and leave to cool. Pack the peaches firmly down in the jars, placing a kernel in each jar. Add the syrup, seal tightly and sterilize for 30-35 minutes (see page 119). Allow to cool in the water bath; test the seal.

Store in a dry, dark place.

Eat these peaches before spring; they do not keep indefinitely. Good with custard or creamy rice.

Grapefruit in syrup

INGREDIENTS

$7\frac{3}{4}$lb / $3\frac{1}{2}$kg large, juicy grapefruit
$4\frac{1}{2}$ cups / $2\frac{1}{4}$lb / 1kg sugar
$3\frac{1}{2}$ cups / 1 pint 8fl oz / 800ml water

METHOD

Remove the peel and all the pith with a very sharp knife, exposing the juicy flesh of the grapefruit; prise out each individual segment from its enclosing membrane without breaking it; this will take patience and skill.

Place the segments in jars and add their juice (work over a bowl so you do not waste any as you work). Leave enough space in the jars for the syrup.

Add the sugar to the water, bring to the boil while stirring with a wooden spoon and then leave to cool. Add enough syrup to cover the grapefruit, seal the jars carefully and sterilize for 15-20 minutes (see method on page 119).

Keep in a dark and absolutely dry storeroom.

The syrup will make a refreshing drink, while the segments can be added to a citrus fruit salad or mixed fruit salad with a little lemon juice.

Plums in syrup

INGREDIENTS

$4\frac{1}{2}$lb / 2kg sound, small plums (Mirabelles or damsons)
1 quart / $1\frac{3}{4}$ pints / 1 litre cooking liquid from the plums
1lb / 450g sugar
1 lemon

METHOD

Wipe the plums with a slightly damp cloth. Prick each one in 5-6 places with a needle, place in a large bowl and cover with boiling water. Leave to stand until the water is lukewarm.

Take the plums from the water, reserving the specified quantity for the sugar syrup.

Spread out the plums on paper towels to dry in the sun or in a warm, well ventilated place. When they are dry, pack into the jars. Make the sugar syrup: mix the sugar into the cooking liquid, bring to the boil and pour immediately over the plums, so the level comes three-quarters of the way up the jars.

Squeeze a few drops of lemon juice into each jar. Seal tightly and sterilize for about 15 minutes (see page 119). Store in a cool, dark place.

Any small plums with fairly thick skins and firm flesh will bottle well, but Mirabelles are probably best for this recipe.

Rhubarb in syrup

INGREDIENTS

4½lb / 2kg cleaned, trimmed pink tender rhubarb

3 cups / 1½lb / 700g sugar

1 lemon

a few slivers fresh (green) ginger root

METHOD

Cut the rhubarb into 2½in / 4cm lengths. Bring a large pan of water acidulated with the juice of the lemon (reserve a few thinly pared pieces of peel) to the boil. As soon as it boils, add the rhubarb; if you are making a large quantity, blanch it in batches. As soon as the water returns to the boil, remove the rhubarb and drain well (reserve the cooking liquid). Dry on paper towels and pack into jars neatly. Place a piece of lemon peel and a thin slice of ginger in each jar.

Make the sugar syrup: stir the sugar into 1 quart / 1¾ pints / 1 litre of the reserved cooking liquid; boil for 2 minutes. Pour straight into the jars, to come just over three-quarters of the way up the rhubarb.

Seal the jars tightly and sterilize for 30-35 minutes (see page 119). Keep in a cool, dark place.

As a pie filling, made into a fool with custard and whipped cream, or on its own with a little pouring cream, rhubarb is an economical and tasty treat.

Grapes in syrup

INGREDIENTS

7¾lb / 3½kg white or black grapes

4 cups / 2lb / 900g sugar

1½ quarts / 2 pints 13fl oz / 1½litres water

1 lemon (peel only)

a few young, tender vine leaves if available

METHOD

Rinse the perfectly sound bunches of ripe grapes briefly under cold running water. Use scissors to snip off each grape, leaving only a millimetre of stem attached to each one. Allowing for wastage, damaged grapes and stalks, you should have 6½lb / 3kg. Spread them out to dry in the sun or a warm place, on a clean cloth, for about 1 hour.

Meanwhile, prepare the sugar syrup: boil the water with the sugar and a piece of lemon peel; boil for 2 minutes and then leave to cool.

Transfer the grapes carefully to jars, making sure you include none which have split skins. Add a piece of lemon peel to each jar and, if available, a couple of rinsed and dried vine leaves. Pour in the syrup to come three-quarters of the way up the jar. Seal tightly and sterilize for 15-20 minutes (see page 119). Keep in a dry, dark place.

Make sure you use grapes with relatively tough skins, which have not been sprayed recently with insecticides (the Italia or Regina varieties are suitable).

Fruit
preserved in spirits and liqueurs

Fruit and liqueurs: the ideal way
to mingle tastes and aromas,
reducing the strength of the alcohol
while strengthening the delicate fragrance of the fruit;
the chance to give your guests
a really unusual after-dinner drink.

Apricots Charterhouse style

INGREDIENTS

- *4½lb / 2kg sound, ripe but firm apricots*
- *4½ cups / 2¼lb / 1kg sugar*
- *1 lemon (all peel, juice of ½)*
- *3 cloves*
- *small piece cinnamon bark*
- *2 cups / 18fl oz / 500ml 50° brandy or marc*
- *1½ quarts / 2 pints 13fl oz / 1½ litres water*

METHOD

Wipe the apricots with a slightly damp cloth and prick each one with a needle in 6-8 places. Boil the sugar and water together for 5-6 minutes, add the apricots and poach gently for 2 minutes. Remove from the heat and leave to stand for at least 8 hours.

When this steeping time is up, drain off all the syrup and boil it gently for 5 minutes before adding the apricots once more. Cover and leave to cool for a few hours.

Drain the apricots and arrange in the jars. Return the syrup to the heat and simmer until it has thickened slightly but is still sufficient to cover three-quarters of the apricots in their jars. Pour over the apricots when just warm. Leave to cool, add a few pieces of lemon peel and a clove to each jar, and some of the lemon juice. Top up with the spirit. Seal the jars and keep in a cool, dark place.

They will be ready to eat after about 3 weeks.

The mildly alcoholic syrup makes a very good summer drink on the rocks.

Apricots in Marsala

INGREDIENTS

- *6½lb / 3kg sound, barely ripe apricots*
- *2½ cups / 1¼lb / 600g sugar*
- *1¾ cups / 14fl oz / 400ml water*
- *2 cups / 18fl oz / 500ml dry Marsala wine*
- *1 lemon*
- *2 cloves*
- *pinch ground cinnamon*

METHOD

Boil the water with the sugar for a few minutes. Remove from the heat, add the Marsala (Madeira can be used if the Sicilian fortified wine is not to hand), a few pieces of lemon peel and the juice, the cinnamon and the cloves. Leave to cool.

Rinse the apricots briefly under the cold tap, then spread to dry out of doors or on paper towels. Cut them in half along their natural groove, pit/stone and pack into the jars. Pour in the cooled Marsala syrup to come three-quarters of the way up the apricots, stopping about 1in / 2-3cms short of the top of the jar. Seal well and sterilize for 10 minutes (see page 119).

Store in a cool, dry place.

The syrup from these preserves turns into the most heavenly drink, while the apricots could be served with zabaglione sauce or in a flan or tartlets.

Apricots in alcohol

INGREDIENTS

4½lb / 2kg barely ripe apricots
1¾ cups / 14oz / 400g sugar
2 cups / 18fl oz / 500ml 90° spirit alcohol (brandy, marc, vodka)
2 cups / 18fl oz / 500ml water
1 lemon (peel only)

METHOD

Boil the water with the sugar and lemon peel. As soon as it comes to the boil, add the apricots (wiped and pierced as in recipe on page 79). Simmer very gently for 5 minutes. Drain well, pack into jars and leave to cool.

Strain the cooking liquid through a fine sieve or cheesecloth/muslin, making up a mixture of half alcohol, half syrup (or with a smaller proportion of spirits, according to taste). Pour over the apricots so that they are covered. Seal and keep in a cool, dark place.

If preferred, just use alcohol on its own: arrange the halved, pitted/stoned raw apricots in layers, alternating with layers of sugar, and fill with the spirit of your choice.

Morello cherries in rum

INGREDIENTS

2¼lb / 1kg ripe but firm Morello cherries
generous cup / 9oz / 250g sugar
a few pieces cinnamon bark
1 lemon (peel only)
2 cups / 18fl oz / 500ml rum (preferably Bacardi)
1 cup / 9fl oz / 250ml liqueur alcohol

METHOD

Rinse the cherries and dry on paper towels very thoroughly. Remove the stems or snip them off to within ¼in / 3mm of the fruit. Pack into a large glass jar or several smaller ones. Distribute the sugar and small pieces of cinnamon between the jars, adding a piece of lemon peel to each.

Pour in the rum until it comes to within ¾in / 2cm of the top of the fruit; top with liqueur alcohol to cover the cherries. Seal tightly and leave in a warm room, preferably in full sunlight, for a week, turning the jar round a little each day and carefully up-ending it to help the sugar spread and dissolve; put away in a cool, dark place. Ready to eat after 4 weeks.

When drained, these cherries are excellent on their own at the end of a meal, or as decoration on trifles or gâteaux; use the alcohol to soak the trifle sponges, or drink it as a liqueur.

Morellos with purée in rum

INGREDIENTS

5½lb / 2½kg sound, ripe Morello cherries
scant cup / 7oz / 200g sugar
1 lemon
2 cups / 18fl oz / 500ml rum

METHOD

Wash the cherries and reserve about 1lb / 500g of the ripest, softest ones. Remove the stalks from all the rest and pack in jars to within ¾in / 2cm of the top.

Sieve the 1lb / 500g of reserved soft cherries; stir the sugar into this purée, together with the lemon juice and a few thin parings of lemon peel. Stir until the sugar has dissolved.

Pour into the jars containing the cherries and then top up with rum. Seal and keep in a cool and dark place without disturbing them until they are eaten.

Cinnamon (small pieces of bark) or cloves can be used instead of lemon peel for extra flavour. Wait a month before tasting; the resulting very strong liqueur can be served with coffee after a meal.

Morello cherries in alcohol

INGREDIENTS

2¼lb / 1kg sound, ripe Morello cherries
scant cup / 7oz / 200g sugar
2 cups / 18fl oz / 500ml alcohol (such as alkermes or maraschino)
small piece cinnamon bark
2-3 cloves
2-3 bitter almonds or apricot kernels

METHOD

Snip off the stalks about ⅛in / 3mm from each cherry; rinse briefly under the cold tap and dry carefully on paper towels. Spread out on fresh towels to dry completely. Pack into jars, add the sugar, cinnamon, cloves and bitter almonds or apricot kernels, and pour in sufficient alcohol to cover the cherries completely. Seal well and keep in a dry, dark place. The cherries will be at their best after 3 months.

The brilliant red of the French or Italian spiced cordial, alkermes, enhances both the taste and appearance of these cherries, which are very useful when decorating desserts, ice-creams and Bavarois cream moulds.

Pineapple in kirsch

INGREDIENTS

5 sound, firm pineapples
2½ cups / 1¼lb / 600g sugar
1 lemon
1 quart / 1¾ pints / 1 litre kirsch
2 quarts / 3½ pints / 2 litres water

METHOD

Use a very sharp knife to peel the pineapple; slice into rounds, remove the hard core and cut into smallish chunks; spread these out on a large plate and sprinkle with the lemon juice.

Bring the sugar and water to the boil; add the pineapple and blanch for a few seconds. Remove the pineapple from the syrup, draining well and leave to cool. Pack into jars, with a piece of lemon peel in each; pour in enough kirsch to cover. If you do not have enough kirsch, top up with a sugar syrup, made by bringing 1⅓ cups / 11oz / 300g sugar and scant ½ cup / 3½oz / 100g water to the boil without stirring. Remove from the heat a few seconds after it has boiled.

Seal the jars tightly; store in a cool, dark place.

Chill the liquid which was used for blanching the pineapple; it is delicious as a drink.

Oranges in alcohol

INGREDIENTS

1lb / 500g ripe, juicy sweet oranges
1¾ cups / 14oz / 400g sugar
2½ cups / 1 pint / 600ml 95° alcohol (brandy, marc, vodka)
1 lemon (peel only)
3 cloves
small piece cinnamon bark

METHOD *(see illustrated instructions on page 189)*

Rub the oranges well with a coarse cloth, pierce each fruit in several places with a large needle and place in a large, wide-necked preserving jar. Pour in the sugar, add the cloves, a few thin pieces of lemon peel and the small piece of cinnamon bark.

Pour in the alcohol so that it completely covers the oranges and seal the jar tightly. Holding the jar horizontally, shake it from side to side to help the sugar start dissolving. Put away in a cool, dry storeroom or larder; during the next six weeks shake the jar from time to time – about once a week will do.

Although these oranges will be at their best after six weeks, you can use them as a dessert after two weeks, but you will need to add a little more sugar. The liquid is very potent and makes a splendid finish to a meal as a digestive liqueur.

Oranges in grappa or marc

INGREDIENTS

2½lb / 1.1kg sound, firm and ripe oranges
1¼ cups / 11oz / 300g sugar
2-3 cloves
a few small pieces cinnamon bark
a sufficient quantity of grappa or marc (rough brandy)

METHOD

You must be quite sure to buy oranges which have not been treated with diphenyl. Wash well under cold running water and dry. Do not peel but, using a very sharp, pointed knife, cut each orange into 6-8 segments or wedges, slicing vertically from top to bottom.

Pack these wedges into jars, arranging them neatly to fit in as many as possible. Add the sugar (an equal quantity to each jar), and place a couple of cloves and a piece of cinnamon in each. Pour in enough grappa (marc made from the skins and stalks of grapes) or brandy to cover the orange segments.

Make sure the seal of the jars is airtight and keep in a cool, dark place. Ready to eat after about 4 weeks.

Usually these segments are placed on cakes or desserts as an alluring decoration. The liquid makes a good liqueur.

Sweet chestnuts in kirsch

INGREDIENTS

2¾lb / 1.2kg Spanish (sweet) chestnuts
generous 1¼ cups / 11oz / 300g sugar
scant ½ cup / 3½fl oz / 100ml water
½ lemon
2 cups / 18fl oz / 500ml kirsch

METHOD

Boil the chestnuts in their shells in plenty of water; peel while still hot, as soon as they can be handled, removing as much of the thin inner skin as possible without breaking them. Place carefully in jars.

Boil the water with the sugar for just as long as it takes to melt the sugar; remove from the heat and add the peel (no pith) and juice of the half lemon; leave to cool. Mix in the kirsch and pour this mixture into the jars, covering the chestnuts completely. Make sure the jars are sealed so that they are airtight and keep in a cool, dark place.

Select very large, plump chestnuts for preserving. These are delicious when served with a topping of whipped cream.

Chestnut rum balls

INGREDIENTS

1lb / 500g sound sweet chestnuts
scant cup / 7oz / 200g sugar
3/2 tablespoons cocoa powder (unsweetened)
1 lemon (peel only)
pinch ground cinnamon
a few drops vanilla extract/essence
¼ cup / 2fl oz / 50ml water
¼ cup / 2fl oz / 50ml rum

METHOD

Cook and peel the chestnuts as directed in the previous recipe; push through a sieve into a heavy saucepan while still warm (this quantity should yield about 11oz / 300g of purée). Dissolve ¼ cup / 2oz / 50g of the sugar in the water and stir into the warm chestnut purée; beat in the sieved cocoa powder, the rum, vanilla and grated lemon peel. Make sure there are no lumps. Bring the purée to a gentle boil while stirring continuously; it should become very thick and smooth. Remove from the heat.

As soon as the mixture is no longer too hot to handle, break off pieces about the size of a hazelnut and roll into balls between the palms of your hands before rolling in the remaining sugar mixed with the ground cinnamon to coat. If necessary, warm the mixture through a little if it becomes too cool to mould easily.

Spread the rum balls out on greaseproof paper or vegetable parchment to dry for a couple of days (outside in the sun or in a warm, well-ventilated place). Store in tins to keep free from moisture.

These chestnut bonbons can be eaten just like any other sweets or candies or used to decorate cakes and desserts.

Cherries in grappa

INGREDIENTS

2¼lb / 1kg sound, firm-fleshed cherries
1¾ cups / 14oz / 400g sugar
½ cup / 4fl oz / 125ml water
a sufficient quantity of grappa, aquavit or other type of marc
1 lemon (peel only)
4-6 small, young cherry leaves

METHOD

Wash the cherries and dry in a cloth; snip off the stalks to within about ⅙in (1mm) of the cherry; spread out to dry completely on paper towels in a well-ventilated place. Pack into jars.

Make a sugar syrup by boiling the sugar and water for about 3 minutes; leave to cool and pour equal quantities into the jars containing the cherries. Top up with good quality grappa, covering the cherries. Add a twist of lemon peel and a few cherry leaves to each jar before sealing. Keep in a dry, dark place.

Try to wait at least 3 months before tasting to give the cherries time to become permeated by the alcohol. If you wish to enchance the flavour of the liquid, add a bitter almond to each jar.

Stuffed figs in brandy

INGREDIENTS

6½lb / 3kg ripe, firm-fleshed figs
6½ cups / 3¼lb / 1½kg sugar
3 cups / 11oz / 300g walnuts (whole, shelled)
2 lemons
brandy as required
water as required

METHOD

Rinse the whole figs briefly but thoroughly under cold running water, spread out on a cloth and dry in the sun for about 1 hour. Slice each fig lengthwise in half leaving the two halves attached and "hinged", press a walnut half into the centre of each side of the fig, convex side downwards, and close the fruit halves together. Pack the figs neatly and fairly tightly into jars in layers. Sprinkle each layer with sugar (make sure you allow a sufficient and even quantity for each layer and jar), a few drops of lemon juice and a piece of peel, and 2-3 tablespoons brandy. When the jar is filled to within ½in / 1cm of its neck (but no more), add a few tablespoonfuls of boiled water to make sure there is plenty of syrup when the figs are ready to eat.

Seal the jars and sterilize for 45 minutes (see page 119). Store in a dry, dark place.

You may wish to be more generous with the brandy. These figs are wonderful with coffee; they also go well with small pastries, petits fours or as a decoration for gâteaux.

Dried figs in grappa

INGREDIENTS

3¼lb / 1½kg dried figs
3¼ cups / 1lb 10oz / 750g sugar
3 cups / 11oz / 300g walnuts (quartered, shelled)
a sufficient quantity of grappa, marc or rum

METHOD

Cut the figs in half and push a quarter walnut into each; press the two halves back together again. Pack the figs neatly into jars in layers. Sprinkle each layer with a tablespoon of sugar and about ¼ cup / 2fl oz / 50ml grappa, marc or rum. Close the jars and leave to stand for a few days; the figs will absorb the spirit and plump out nicely. Open the jars and add more of your chosen spirit, enough to completely cover the figs. Seal and keep in a dry, dark place.

You can either use good quality commercially dried figs or dry them yourself in the oven. In hot dry climates they can, of course, be dried in the sun by threading a piece of string through their stalks and hanging them to dry in the open air.

Mixed berry fruit salad in alcohol

Mixed berry fruit salad in alcohol

INGREDIENTS

1lb / 500g raspberries or loganberries
½lb / 250g redcurrants
½lb / 250g bilberries
4½ cups / 2¼lb / 1kg sugar
a sufficient quantity of sweet liqueur

METHOD

Remove any stray leaves or stalks from the fruit, but do not wash. If possible, the fruit should have been picked by being snipped off with scissors and the stalks trimmed down to within a fraction of the actual berry; the green calyx on the fruits should also be snipped off with small pointed scissors.

Arrange layers of each different type of fruit, sprinkling each layer with plenty of sugar (e.g. a layer of blueberries, sugar, redcurrants, sugar, raspberries and so on). Do not crush the fruit and keep it as intact as possible.

Pour in sufficient alcohol to come 1in / 2½cm above the fruit; close the jars tightly and leave to macerate for 2 months in a cool, dark cellar or storeroom.

This steeped fruit salad should be served in small quantities, in tiny coffee cups to round off a dinner party menu. Or spoon over ice-cream coupes or sundaes.

Jujubes in alcohol

INGREDIENTS

1lb / 450g jujubes
scant cup / 7oz / 200g sugar
½ lemon (peel only)
small piece vanilla pod, crushed
1½ cups / 14fl oz / 400ml 95° spirits (brandy or marc)

METHOD

Pare off the lemon peel thinly, leaving all the pith behind, and cut into very thin strips. Wipe the jujubes with a slightly damp cloth and pack into a jar (capacity of approx 2-2½lb / 1kg); add the sugar, scant ½ cup / 3½fl oz / 100ml alcohol, the lemon peel and vanilla, and seal the jar so that it is air-tight. Leave to stand in full sun on a windowsill, shaking gently and turning the jar upside down from time to time until the sugar has completely dissolved. Open the jar, pour in the remaining alcohol, seal tightly once more and put away in a cool cellar.

Leave for at least 6 months, after which the jujubes will have matured and be ready to use. By this time, the liquid surrounding the jujubes will be about 42° strength.

Jujube berries (which gave the candies/sweets their name) are usually ripe in late July and August. When preserved in this way they have a distinctive and pleasant flavour. They can be drained and used to decorate desserts and ice-cream, and the liquid makes an excellent drink.

Pears in grappa or marc

Blueberries/bilberries with maraschino

INGREDIENTS

- *2¼lb / 1kg sound bluberries/bilberries*
- *4½ cups / 2¼lb / 1kg sugar*
- *1 lemon*
- *1 cup / 9fl oz / 250ml maraschino*

METHOD

Remove any stalks or leaves from the berries, but do not wash; they should be absolutely dry. Mix with the sugar, stirring and turning very gently with a wooden spoon. Transfer the berries and sugar into jars, add the strained juice of the lemon and a few pieces of peel. Place the lids on the jars and leave to stand for 24 hours.

When this time is up, pour in enough maraschino to completely cover the berries. Seal the jars so that they are airtight and over the next 7 days leave them out in the sun or on a sunny windowsill for 2 hours each day, turning them upside down a few times to blend the sugar and liqueur. As the berries steep they impart the most exquisite flavour and aroma to the maraschino, making a fairly thick syrup which will have an alcoholic content of about 14°. When you have completed the above procedure, store in a cool, dry place.

Serve as the finishing touch to a meal, as you would morello or black cherries preserved in brandy or some other type of alcohol, or use to top a dessert or mix into a fruit salad. Dilute the syrup with iced water or seltzer, soda water or sparkling mineral water for a refreshing drink.

Pears in grappa or marc

INGREDIENTS

- *20 small cooking pears*
- *scant ¾lb / 11oz / 300g cube/lump sugar*
- *1 lemon*
- *3¼ cups / 1¼ pints / 750ml very good quality grappa or marc*

METHOD

Peel the pears but do not core them or remove the stalks; as you peel them, place in a large bowl of water acidulated with the juice of the lemon to prevent them discolouring.

Place the sugar cubes/lumps in a heavy bottomed casserole dish (fireproof) and add enough water to barely cover. Heat gently until the sugar has dissolved. When the resulting syrup is quite thick, place the pears carefully in it and simmer over a very low heat until they are tender and appear almost translucent. Test with the point of a sharp knife – it should slide into the flesh easily. Pack one by one into preserving jars.

Pour the grappa into the syrup, stir and then pour into the jars containing the pears. Seal, leave to cool and then put away in a cool, dark place.

Use for dessert coupes or sundaes, or serve just as they are at the end of a meal with a little of their syrup.

Jujubes in alcohol

Peaches in liqueur

INGREDIENTS

- *2¼lb / 1kg sound, firm, ripe peaches*
- *4½ cups / 2¼lb / 1kg sugar*
- *1 lemon*
- *sweet liqueur (alkermes, maraschino, Grand Marnier) as required*

METHOD

Wash the peaches well; blanch for a moment in boiling water, plunge into cold water and peel. Slice in half and pit/stone. Sprinkle the cut surfaces with a little lemon juice as you slice them in half to prevent them turning brown.

Arrange in jars, alternating layers of peaches with layers of sugar; as you fill the jar, pour in the alcohol, tapping the base of the jar gently to ensure that there are no air pockets. Leave at least ¼-½in / 1cm between the top of the fruit and alcohol and the lid.

Seal the jars; make sure they are airtight and store in a well-ventilated, dry, dark place.

The fruit will be at its best 3 months later. You could add a bitter almond and a clove or two to each jar for extra flavour, or a few tender young peach leaves. Drink the liqueur-flavoured syrup with your coffee at the end of a dinner party. You can mix these peaches with fresh fruit salad.

Blackcurrants in grappa or marc

INGREDIENTS

- *3¼lb / 1½kg sound, barely ripe blackcurrants*
- *scant cup / 7oz / 200g sugar*
- *1 quart / 1¾ pints / 1 litre good quality grappa, aquavit or other type of marc*

METHOD

Rinse the blackcurrants in cold water; take off their stalks carefully, trying to split as few skins as possible. Spread out on paper towels to dry. Transfer to preserving jars, sprinkling with the sugar; top up with enough grappa or other type of good quality marc to just cover. Seal the jars and keep in cool, dark storage.

Allow 2 months to pass before trying these; serve at the end of a meal or use as a topping and decoration for glass coupes of fruit salad.

Grapes in grappa

Plums in aquavit or marc

INGREDIENTS

- *2¼lb / 1kg sound, small, firm-fleshed plums*
- *a sufficient quantity of sugar*
- *scant quart / approx 1½ pints / scant litre aquavit, brandy or marc*
- *1 vanilla pod*
- *1 lemon (peel only)*
- *4/3 teaspoons tea*
- *1 teaspoon peppermint tea*
- *2 cups / 18fl oz / 500ml water*

METHOD

Boil the water and pour straight on to the tea leaves and peppermint tea; leave to brew for at least 5 minutes as it must be strong. When the mixed tea is lukewarm add the washed and dried plums and leave to stand for about 4-5 hours, stirring occasionally very gently. The plums will become permeated with the flavour of the tea.

Remove the plums with a slotted/perforated spoon and pierce each one in 5 or 6 places with a needle.

Pack into preserving jars, add a few pieces of vanilla pod to each one, together with a small piece of lemon peel and a few teaspoons of sugar. Pour in enough aquavit or marc to cover the plums. Seal and keep cool and dry, well away from light.

Pick the plums when they are really ripe (September-October) to be sure of having them with plenty of flavour and sweetness. You can eat these plums after only three weeks; serve for dessert.

Grapes in grappa

INGREDIENTS

- *2¼lb / 1kg sound, white grapes*
- *a few small pieces vanilla pod*
- *a few small pieces cinnamon bark*
- *1 lemon (peel only)*
- *approx 1 quart / 1¾ pints / 1 litre grappa or other type of marc*

METHOD *(see illustrated instructions on page 190)*

Carefully snip off each grape from the bunch, leaving a fraction (about 1 millimetre) of stalk attached; rinse in cold water, drain and spread out on paper towels or a cloth to dry. Transfer to preserving jars; place a small piece of vanilla pod in each, together with a small piece of cinnamon stick and a twist of thinly pared lemon peel. Add enough grappa or marc (use the best quality available) to cover the grapes and seal the jars very tightly. Put away in your store cupboard and wait at least a month before tasting.

Dates, prunes and all sorts of dried fruits can be processed in this way.

This is such a simple preserve to make and yet it is quite delicious as the final course after an elaborate or copious meal.

Grapes in liqueur

INGREDIENTS

4½lb / 2kg thick-skinned, large white grapes
generous 1lb / 500g sugar
scant ½ cup / 3½fl oz / 100ml water
1 lemon (peel only)
1 quart / 1¾ pints / 1 litre dessert alcohol or liqueur of your choice (45° strength)

METHOD

Snip the grapes off the bunch, leaving a fraction of stalk attached to each one. Rinse in cold water and then dry thoroughly before placing carefully in jars without crushing.

Make the syrup by boiling the sugar and water together until the sugar has completely dissolved. Leave to cool completely. Pour into the jars, allowing an equal volume for each one, and then top up with the alcohol or chosen liqueur so that the grapes are covered. Place a piece of lemon peel in each jar for extra flavour. Make sure the jars are airtight and then put away in a cool, dark place.

The Regina and Italia varieties of grapes are best for this treatment; they are rather elongated in shape, firm and very sweet. Be ruthless in discarding any blemished or damaged grapes: they must be perfect or they will not keep.

Sweet-sour cherries

INGREDIENTS

2¼lb / 1kg ripe black cherries
generous cup / 9fl oz / 250g sugar
1 quart / 1¾ pint / 1 litre white wine vinegar
10 cloves
1 lemon (peel only)

METHOD

Wash the cherries and then snip the stalks to within a fraction of an inch (about 1 millimetre) of the cherry itself. Dry, then pierce each one in two or three places with a needle and place in jars.

Heat the vinegar with the sugar, cloves and a few pieces of lemon peel (make sure there is no white pith attached) and boil for 15 minutes. Remove from the heat and leave to cool until lukewarm. Strain and pour over the cherries. Seal tightly and keep in a cool, dark place.

Wait at least a month before trying the cherries to give them time to macerate in their sweet-sour liquid. Serve in much the same way as whole cranberry sauce, with boiled or poached meats or poultry, roast duck or turkey, or make this an unusual appetizer to serve with drinks as you would olives.

Cherries in spiced vinegar

INGREDIENTS

6½lb / 3kg sound, firm cherries (black or Dukes)
scant ½ cup / 3½oz / 100g sugar
10 small, tender cherry leaves
2 cloves
small piece cinnamon bark
pinch ground ginger
2½ quarts / 4½ pints / 2½ litres best red or white wine vinegar

METHOD

Wash and dry the cherries; snip the stalks to within a fraction of an inch (about 1 millimetre) of the fruits; blanch a few at a time only, to allow the water to return to the boil almost immediately after they are added to it. Take out as soon as the water has boiled and spread out on a cloth to dry. Blanch the cherry leaves if used.

Heat the vinegar very gently with the sugar and spices until the sugar has dissolved, but do not let it boil. Remove from the heat and leave to cool while packing the cherries into jars methodically to fit in as many as possible; place a cherry leaf here and there among them. Strain the lukewarm vinegar and pour into the jars. Seal and keep in a cool, dark place.

Serve these spiced cherries whenever you would normally serve olives, for cocktail snacks or with special salads. They also go well with boiled and poached meat or poultry.

Marinated pears

INGREDIENTS

6½lb / 3kg firm, ripe Kaiser (or Comice or Williams) pears
1½ cups / 14fl oz / 400ml white or red wine vinegar
2½ cups / 1¼lb / 600g sugar
8 cloves
5 juniper berries
5 peppercorns
1 teaspoon ground cinnamon
3 lemons
5 quarts / 8½ pints / 5 litres water
pinch salt

METHOD

Peel the pears, quarter and core, dropping them straight into cold water containing the juice of a lemon.

Bring the water to the boil with scant cup / 7oz / 200g of the sugar and the juice of another lemon. Add the pears to the boiling liquid and blanch for 2 minutes, then remove and drain on cloths, leaving them in full sunlinght for 1-2 days until they have dried and are partially dehydrated. Reserve 1 quart / 1¾ pints / 1 litre of the cooking liquid.

Pack the sun-dried pears into jars; boil the vinegar and all the spices and flavourings with the remaining sugar and the peel and juice of the last lemon for 2 minutes, then leave to cool completely. Strain and pour over the pears; if there is not enough marinade to cover them, add a little of the reserved light syrup left over from blanching the pears. Seal the jars and store in a cool, dark place.

Russian housewives used to pride themselves on these home-preserved pears, which go very well with roast game.

Peaches in spiced mild vinegar

INGREDIENTS

2¼lb / 1kg sound, firm ripe peaches
4½ cups / 2¼lb / 1kg sugar
2 cups / 18fl oz / 500ml good white wine vinegar
1 lemon
5 cloves
small piece cinnamon stick

METHOD

Immerse the peaches for a second or two in very hot water, drain and refresh in cold water to make them easier to peel; cut in half (or quarters if very large), sprinkling with a little lemon juice to prevent discolouration. Put them into prepared jars.

Boil the vinegar with the spices and sugar for about 10 minutes until reduced and somewhat thickened (estimate how much you will need to cover the peaches and do not reduce too much). Strain the spiced, sweetened vinegar, discarding the spices, before pouring into the jars to cover the peaches. Seal tightly and keep in a dry, dark place.

This is a very unusual preserve which must be tried to realize just how delicious it really is. Exquisite with boiled or poached meat, chicken or roast duck.

Sweet-sour plums

INGREDIENTS

6½lb / 3kg small plums (preferably Burbank)
4½ cups / 2¼lb / 1kg sugar
1½ level teaspoons ground cinnamon
1 lemon
1 quart / 1¾ pints / 1 litre white wine vinegar
5-6 cloves

METHOD

Wash the plums; do not remove the stalks.

Bring the vinegar to the boil with all the other ingredients before adding the whole plums. Boil for 5 minutes, remove from the heat and leave the plums to stand in the liquid for about 5-6 hours. Afterwards, drain the plums, transfer to another non-metallic dish or pan and boil the liquid again for 10 minutes. Pour over the plums and leave to stand for another 5-6 hours. Repeat this procedure (handling the plums very delicately on each occasion) until the spiced liquid has boiled down to a sufficient volume to just cover the plums when packed in their jars (you can estimate this approximately).

When the plums are packed into the jars, bring the liquid to the boil for the last time; strain and pour while hot over the plums to cover them completely. Seal the jars tightly when cold and store in a cool, dark place.

Very good as an unusual starter or alternatively with boiled meats or full-flavoured sausages. Marvellous with grilled/broiled chicken.

Candied and dried fruit

Candied, crystallized and dried fruits
can easily be prepared at home.
Besides fruit and sugar,
the only ingredients needed
are patience
and a little free time.

Candied/crystallized orange peel

Candied/crystallized apricots

INGREDIENTS

- *2¼lb / 1kg net weight sound, ripe apricots (pitted/stoned)*
- *1 lemon*
- *3½ cups / 1¾lb / 800g sugar*
- *1½ quarts / 2 pints 13fl oz / 1½ litres water*
- *1 tablespoon glucose syrup*

METHOD

Place the apricot halves in a pan, cover with the water, the lemon juice and 6-7/4-5 tablespoons sugar. Bring to the boil and simmer for a minute or two; drain off and reserve all the cooking liquid. Set the apricots aside in a fairly shallow dish. Return the reserved liquid to the pan with the remaining sugar and boil until all the sugar has dissolved; pour the syrup over the apricots while still warm and leave to stand for 24 hours. Drain off all the syrup again, boil in the pan so that it thickens further and then pour over the apricots once more and leave to stand for another 24 hours.

Repeat this process another 4 times, by which time the syrup should have reached the "large thread" stage, that is 219°F / 104°C or 38° Baumé (see below), leaving the fruit to soak in the syrup each time for 24 hours and adding the glucose to the final syrup. Store the apricots in glass jars.

A quick way to test for "large thread" thickness of the syrup is to place a drop between your thumb and forefinger: when you pull them apart slowly a thread of sugar syrup should remain suspended, linking them.

Candied/crystallized orange peel

INGREDIENTS

- *scant ½lb / 200g peel from scrubbed, washed oranges*
- *scant ½ cup / 3½ oz / 100g sugar*

METHOD

Peel the oranges, preferably in quarters, and remove all the pith from the rind. Cut into fairly large pieces or into thin strips. Place in a pan, add the sugar and just enough water to cover. Bring slowly to the boil and simmer very gently for about 10 minutes. Remove from the heat and leave to stand in the pan for 24 hours. Return to the heat, adding a little more sugar and water if necessary to cover the peel; boil slowly again for about 15 minutes. Remove from the heat and leave to stand for another 24 hours. Remove the peel from the syrup with a slotted or perforated spoon, letting as much syrup drip back into the pan as possible. Boil the syrup for 5 minutes. Turn off the heat. Return the peel to the syrup and leave to stand for 24 hours more. After this, return to the boil and cook until the peel looks almost translucent. Remove from the heat and take the peel out of the pan; spread the pieces out to dry, making sure they are not touching each other. Leave for a day and then roll them in a little superfine/caster sugar. They will keep for a long time in glass jars.

Various fruit cakes call for candied peel; they can also be used for certain Italian pastry fillings and to decorate cakes.

Marrons glacés

INGREDIENTS

1¾lb / 800g large, sound sweet (Spanish) chestnuts
3½ cups / 1¾lb / 800g sugar
1½ cups / 14fl oz / 400ml water
1 tablespoon light corn syrup/glucose syrup

METHOD

Preparing marrons glacés is quite straightforward: all you need is plenty of patience and a little skill. Boil the chestnuts in abundant water. While they are cooking boil the sugar, water and glucose in a pan wide enough to accommodate all the chestnuts in a single layer. As soon as the syrup comes to the boil, turn off the heat (the syrup should remain lukewarm throughout the procedure outlined below). When the chestnuts are cooked, peel off the outer and inner skins as soon as they are no longer too hot to handle; if they cool too much this will become difficult. Care must be taken when peeling as they break easily; a few may break however delicately you go about it, but you should finish with just over 1lb / 500g whole peeled chestnuts. Lower them one by one into the warm syrup, cover the pan with its lid and leave to stand for 24 hours.

The following day, heat the syrup with the chestnuts over a very low heat; when hot enough to have turned the syrup liquid again, remove from the heat. Use a fork to lift the chestnuts one by one out of the syrup and place on a cake rack over a shallow tray to collect drips of syrup. Return the syrup to the boil for 2 minutes. Remove from the heat and carefully replace the chestnuts. Cover and leave to stand for another 24 hours. Then repeat the operation, but after removing the chestnuts from the syrup, boil it for 3-4 minutes to thicken; replace the chestnuts in the syrup while it is still hot and let stand for another day. Repeat this process twice more; see that the sugar syrup does not become too thick or crystallize (the corn syrup/glucose syrup helps prevent this) or it will not penetrate the chestnuts; you can determine this when it is cold. If so, add a few drops of hot water when it is cool and after you have removed the chestnuts for draining. Finally, heat the pan containing the sugar and chestnuts after they have had their last soaking, remove the chestnuts again with a fork and leave to dry on the rack for 2 days; store in an airtight tin.

Delicious served with whipped cream (flavoured with vanilla and/or rum) or with mascarpone cream (fresh, unripened cream cheese, available in cartons from good Italian grocers). Or they can be chopped and used in fillings.

Candied/crystallized apples

INGREDIENTS

2¼lb / 1kg small, firm apples (such as Russet or Reinette)
5¾ cups / 2lb 14oz / 1.3kg sugar
2 cups / 18fl oz / 500ml water
1 lemon

METHOD

Wipe the apples well with a damp cloth; they should all have their stalks intact. Using a cocktail stick, pierce the flesh, through the skin, in a dozen places.

Choose a pan large enough to contain all the apples in a single layer and boil 2½ cups / 1¼lb / 600g of the sugar with generous 1½ cups / 14fl oz / 400ml water for 2 minutes; remove from the heat and lower the apples quickly into it while still hot. They should fit comfortably into the pan without being squeezed too closely together. Sprinkle with the juice of the lemon. Cover the pan and leave to stand for 24 hours.

The next day, remove the lid and return to the heat. Just before the syrup boils, remove the apples carefully and leave to dry.

Boil the syrup for 5 minutes, then remove from the heat and replace the apples. Cover and leave to stand for a further 24 hours.

Repeat the operation the next day and on 3-4 successive days, or until the syrup is thick and a little darker than honey. The apples should never be left in the syrup once it has come to the boil. They will end up looking somewhat shrunken and wrinkled when processed. Make a fresh sugar syrup by boiling 2½ cups / 1¼lb / 600g sugar with ¼ cup / 2fl oz / 50-60ml water for 2 minutes. Remove the apples from the first syrup, drain and then place in the fresh, hot, thick syrup. Cover and leave to stand for 24 hours. The first syrup can be diluted with a little water and used again to candy other fruits.

The following day, heat the syrup containing the apples, removing them just before it comes to the boil; boil gently to reduce and thicken for about 10 minutes and then quickly return the apples to the pan to coat them, turning them carefully. Remove from the heat, cover and leave for 24 hours. Next day, heat the syrup, take out the apples and place on a clean work surface to dry after coating them with the remaining scant ½ cup / 3½oz / 100g of superfine/caster sugar. Leave for a couple of days in a dry, well-ventilated place.

Once the candying/crystallizing and drying process is complete, store in large glass jars or tins lined with waxed paper or greaseproof paper and keep in a dry cupboard.

Mix with fruit compotes or use as part of the filling for cakes, apple turnovers or puffs.

Candied/crystallized pears

INGREDIENTS

6 small, ripe pears
½ cup / 4oz / 120g sugar

METHOD

Peel, core and quarter the pears. Pour a scant ½ cup / approx 3½ fl oz / 100ml water into a large pan, add the pear quarters and bring to the boil. When the pears are almost tender, remove from the pan and drain well. Place the sugar in a small saucepan, moisten with a few tablespoons of water and bring to the boil over a gentle heat; simmer while stirring until the sugar has completely dissolved; the syrup must not start to colour. Place the pear quarters in the syrup, turn over gently and then remove, placing on a rack under the broiler/grill at a very low heat to dry.

Repeat this procedure 4 times, by which time the pears should be saturated (with the sugar syrup which will become thicker each time it boils). Dry very thoroughly after each immersion. Store in jars.

Surprisingly good as an unusual accompaniment to boiled meats.

Candied/crystallized peaches

INGREDIENTS

11lb / 5kg firm peaches
1 quart / 1¾ pints / 1 litre water
10lb / 4½kg sugar
2 lemons

METHOD

Blanch the peaches by plunging into boiling water for a few seconds, then into cold water. Peel and cut in half, removing the pits/stones (this should yield a net weight of about 8¾lb / 4kg peach halves). Spread out to dry slightly.

Place the sugar, water, peel of one lemon (no pith) and the juice of both lemons in a preserving pan. Stir continuously while heating to help dissolve the sugar. When the syrup reaches boiling point, add the peaches and simmer for a moment or two. Remove from the heat and leave to stand in the syrup in a cool place for 24 hours. Heat the peaches and syrup over a very low heat; remove the peaches with a slotted spoon and transfer to another container.

Bring the syrup to the boil and cook for 3-5 minutes. Remove from the heat and pour over the peaches. Remove the lemon peel. Leave to stand for a further 24 hours. Repeat this process at least 3 more times, until the peaches have absorbed all, or almost all, of the syrup. Warm them up a little to make it easier when removing them from the pan. Spread them out in a single layer on racks which have been covered with greaseproof paper and leave to dry in the sun for 3-5 days, turning them frequently and remembering not to leave them outside at night.

When they have dried and the sugar has crystallized, store away in wooden boxes lined with greaseproof paper.

Splendid for adding a little glamour to ice-cream sundaes.

Candied/crystallized violets

INGREDIENTS

¼lb / 125g violets (stamens, stigma and calyx removed), as fresh and scented as possible
scant 1¾ cups / 13oz / 375g sugar

METHOD

The violets must be absolutely free of dew or other moisture, not at all wilted. Arrange in a jar, alternating layers of violets with a sprinkling of sugar; you should start with a layer of violets and end with a layer of sugar. When the jar is full, seal and leave in a dry, dark place. Check the contents of the jar each day for a week, and if the sugar needs blending with them more thoroughly, stir carefully with a skewer or clean stick. Store the jar, tightly sealed, well away from light.

Use these violets sparingly to flavour and decorate desserts (such as floating islands on a base of crème anglaise); make sure the jar is tightly closed after extracting violets for use. If the sugar shows signs of crystallizing, add a few drops of 95° alcohol, or a little marc or aquavit.

Strictly speaking, these do not qualify for the description of candied or crystallized violets: the method is different but the result exactly the same (if anything, this recipe gives a better scent).

Candied/crystallized pumpkin

INGREDIENTS

4½lb / 2kg firm mature pumpkin
approx 1lb / 500g sugar
2 cups / 18fl oz / 500ml water
1 teaspoon salt

METHOD

Cut the pumpkin in quarters, peel and remove the seeds and membrane. Boil in plenty of water until almost tender but still crisp, with plenty of bite (if at all overdone it will turn mushy later). The cooking times given below are based on the assumption that the gross weight of 4½lb / 2kg will yield as little as 2¼lb / 1kg of flesh.

Make a sugar syrup by mixing the sugar with the salt and water and then boiling for 5 minutes, keeping it hot (but not boiling) until the pumpkin is boiled and drained. Place the pumpkin pieces in the syrup and simmer until the pumpkin is tender and has had time to absorb as much sugar syrup as possible. When the pumpkin is done it will look almost translucent. Remove from the heat and leave to cool in the syrup. When nearly cold, remove the pumpkin pieces with a slotted or perforated spoon and set aside. Boil up the syrup for 2 minutes. Remove from the heat and replace the pumpkin pieces, leaving them to cool once more in the thick syrup. When cold, remove the pumpkin and dry on a rack for 24 hours in a well-ventilated place. Afterwards the quarters can be cut into dice, rhomboids or diamonds and then rolled in sugar. Store in small glass jars.

Add to fillings for pumpkin pies, fritters and tarts as well as savoury pumpkin tortelli (a type of ravioli).

Dried apricots

INGREDIENTS

ripe but not overripe apricots

METHOD

Cut the apricots in half along their natural groove and discard the pits/stones; spread out on oven racks. Leave in a cool oven to dry for a few hours on two successive days. When they all look wizened and wrinkled, spread to dry further out of doors, in full sunlight for 3-4 days (bring them inside in the evening to avoid the dew), discarding any which look mouldy or rotten rather than healthily dried. The objective is for the fruit to lose all its excess moisture quickly without becoming too dry. Cover the apricots loosely with a cloth or greaseproof paper while they are out in the sun. Store in very clean wooden boxes.

When reconstituting the apricots prior to using them, place in a bowl and cover with water or water and wine or liqueur of your choice; leave to stand for 30 minutes to an hour and then cook in the soaking liquid.

Wonderful for French apricot flans or fillings for pastries and pies. You can also purée them when cooked; add a few drops of lemon juice and a little sugar and serve with cream or use as the basic material for a hot apricot soufflé.

Dried apples

INGREDIENTS

sound, ripe apples

METHOD *(see illustrated instructions on page 191)*

Peel the apples, leaving them whole, then use an apple corer to remove the cores. Slice horizontally into rings, which should be about ½in / 1cm thick. Dry in a cool oven (104°F / 40°C), making sure that they only dry rather than cook. Leave them in the oven all day (or all night); spread them out in full sunlight and turn them 2 or 3 times during the day. When they are dried they should still be tender and flexible, not hard and brittle. Remember to bring them in each evening before the dew falls. Store in small, very clean wooden boxes, lined if possible with paper impregnated with sulphur dioxide, or alternatively use greaseproof paper.

When you need to use them, soak overnight in lukewarm water so they reconstitute by re-absorbing the same amount of moisture lost during the drying process. Check that they are all covered by the water while soaking – press down with a saucer and weight if necessary.

They can be cooked in the water used for reconstituting them.

Best served quite simply, as a hot fruit dessert with cream or custard.

Unusual preserves

Here are some novelties,
some out of the ordinary tastes
and textures for the adventurous.
These original and delicious
combinations of fruit, sugar and other flavours
can be stored ready for the day when you
feel like giving a fillip to main courses
or a gourmet touch to home-made
cakes and desserts.

Strawberry sauce

Orange sauce

INGREDIENTS

3 juicy oranges
2 lemons
generous cup / 9oz / 250g sugar
1 cup / 9fl oz / 250ml full-bodied beef or veal gravy
½ cup / 4fl oz / 125ml white wine
¼ cup / 2fl oz / 50ml curaçao
pinch salt
generous pinch pepper

METHOD

Peel off the zest only of the oranges and lemons, leaving the pith behind; cut into very narrow strips and blanch these in lightly salted boiling water. Drain and leave to dry. Bring the sugar and white wine slowly to a gentle boil and cook, over a low heat, stirring very gently occasionally with a wooden spoon until the sugar starts to turn golden yellow; remove from the heat immediately. Add the juice from the oranges and lemons and return to a slow boil over a low heat for 4-5 minutes. Add the meat gravy or rich stock or broth, the strips of lemon and orange peel and simmer, skimming off any scum, for 5 minutes to reduce and slightly thicken the sauce. Season with salt and freshly ground pepper.

If the sauce needs further thickening, stir in a teaspoon of potato flour or arrowroot mixed with a little white wine. When the sauce is ready (about the consistency of light/pouring cream), remove from the heat and stir in the curaçao; pour into jars immediately and seal tightly. Sterilize for about 10 minutes (see page 119). Store in a cool, dark place.

Use for duck à l'orange or serve with turkey.

Cornelian cherry (cornel) sauce

INGREDIENTS

4½lb / 2kg cornelian cherries (cornels)
3½ cups / 1¾lb / 800g sugar
pinch ground cinnamon
1 lemon
1 quart / 1¾ pints / 1 litre water

METHOD

Check and wash the cornels; there is no need to pit/stone them. Place in a preserving pan with the water and the thinly pared peel of half the lemon.

Simmer over a moderate heat for about 2 hours, stirring and removing any scum from time to time. Remove from the heat, leave until just warm and then sieve into a large saucepan. Stir in the sugar, lemon juice and cinnamon. Bring to the boil and cook for about 5 minutes, stirring continuously.

Let the sauce become completely cool before pouring into jars; seal hermetically and store in a dry, dark place.

The pleasantly sharp taste of this sauce lends an extra kick to boiled or poached meat and poultry (beef, capon or pullet, chicken, turkey and calf's head).

Apple sauce

INGREDIENTS

2¼lb / 1kg apples
1 lemon
5 cloves
½ teaspoon ground cinnamon
scant ½ cup / 3½fl oz / 100ml white wine
generous cup / 9oz / 250g sugar
pinch mustard powder (English type)
pinch finely ground white pepper
pinch salt

METHOD

Peel and coarsely chop the apples; place in the preserving pan with the juice of the lemon and a few pieces of peel, the cloves, cinnamon and white wine. Bring to the boil, skimming when necessary; simmer until all the moisture has evaporated and the apples are very tender. Push through a fine hair sieve (discarding the lemon peel and cloves). Return the purée to the pan and stir in the sugar, salt, pepper and mustard powder.

Bring to a gentle boil while stirring continuously and cook until the correct consistency is achieved, as for jam. Pour the hot mixture into clean, absolutely dry jars; seal very tightly and keep in a cool, dark place.

It is a good idea to use small jars, as you will only need a little at a time. Serve with roast pork, and furred or feathered game.

Sweet-sour redcurrant sauce

INGREDIENTS

3¼lb / 1½kg sound, ripe redcurrants
3 cups / 1½lb / 700g sugar
1½ cups / 14fl oz / 400ml best quality white or red wine vinegar
pinch ground cinnamon
2 cloves
1 lemon (peel only)

METHOD

Wash the redcurrants and take them off their stalks, letting them fall into a glass or china bowl. Pour the vinegar over them, adding the cinnamon, cloves and a piece of lemon peel. Leave to stand for about 2 hours, then transfer to a preserving pan; bring to a fast boil and skim, then reduce the heat and simmer for about 15 minutes, stirring continuously.

Add the sugar and continue cooking, very gently, until the mixture is nearly as thick as jam but more syrupy. Remove from the heat and pour straight into jars, sealing tightly and storing in a cool, dark, dry place.

This sauce is a perfect complement to roast game and roast lamb.

Strawberry sauce

INGREDIENTS

2¼lb / 1kg very ripe, sound strawberries
4lb / 1.8kg sugar
1 lemon
1½ quarts / 2 pints 13fl oz / 1½ litres 45° alcohol, such as strawberry liqueur

METHOD

Wash the strawberries only if absolutely necessary. Hull them and mix with the sugar and the juice and grated rind of the lemon in a large, very clean glass or china bowl. Leave to stand in a cool, well-ventilated place for about 2 days, stirring and turning thoroughly at least twice a day with a wooden spatula or spoon; keep the bowl covered with cheesecloth/muslin or mesh to protect from insects.

After 2 days, add the alcohol to the strawberries. Stir well and strain through a jelly bag or fine hair sieve, squeezing or pushing through all the strawberry flesh as well. Pour into small, wide-necked bottles or jars and seal tightly. Store in a cool, dark place.

This sauce or purée gives a wonderful lift to fruit salads and to summer drinks made with plenty of crushed ice; or use as a topping.

Fluffy apple cream

INGREDIENTS

2¼lb / 1kg (net weight) peeled, chopped apples
approx 1lb / 500g sugar
1½ cups / 14fl oz / 400ml water
5 egg whites
1 lemon
¼ cup / 2fl oz / 50ml rum
2 drops vanilla extract/essence

METHOD

Simmer the apples slowly with the water, sugar and the juice and rind of the lemon (leave the pith behind). When the apples are tender, put through a food mill or sieve and return to the preserving pan. Cook while stirring over a low heat until jam consistency is reached. Remove from the heat.

Stir in the vanilla and rum and then beat in the egg whites quickly and vigorously with a balloon whisk (the object is to beat them with the apple mixture and incorporate as much air as possible; if you are not quick enough, the heat of the apple mixture will solidify them).

Continue beating for about 10 minutes, until the mixture is pale, glossy and soft. At this point it should be cool, ready to transfer to small glass jars. Sprinkle the surface of each jar with a layer of sugar: this will crystallize later. Seal the jars tightly and sterilize for 15-20 minutes (see page 119); store in a cool place.

Very good for cake and dessert fillings; it also makes an excellent spread.

Lemon flip and Lemon curd

Lemon flip

INGREDIENTS

scant ½ cup / 3½fl oz / 100ml lemon juice
2 lemons
scant cup / 7oz / 200g sugar
scant cup / 7fl oz / 200ml water, boiling
scant ½ cup / 3½fl oz / 100ml dry Marsala (or other fortified wine, sherry, port, Madeira, etc.)
2 very fresh eggs

METHOD

Pare the lemons carefully, leaving behind all the pith. Cut the peel into thin strips and place in a Pyrex or china bowl with the sugar; pour in the boiling water.

Stir well and leave to cool. When cold, mix in the well-beaten eggs, one at a time, followed by the strained lemon juice and the Marsala. Stir vigorously and then strain.

Pour into bottles or jars and store in the refrigerator or a cool cellar.

Use a hand-held electric beater to whisk the eggs thoroughly. This concoction makes a very good pick-me-up or tonic; it can be heated over hot (not boiling) water in the winter. Serve cold (with ice if wished) during hot weather.

Lemon curd

INGREDIENTS

scant cup / 7oz / 200g butter, softened at room temperature
2lb / 900g sugar
12 very fresh eggs
8 juicy lemons

METHOD

Grate the lemon peel (removing just the yellow zest but none of the pith, which is unpleasantly bitter), into a large double saucepan or bowl over hot water. Add the juice of the lemons, the softened butter and the sugar.

Heat slowly while stirring gently, until the butter has melted and blended with the other ingredients; the mixture should be warm rather than hot, and the water below should not be allowed to boil.

Beat the eggs well and add to the lemon mixture. Continue stirring over a very low heat until the smooth, golden yellow curd thickens; if it comes too close to boiling point it will curdle.

When the mixture coats the back of the wooden spoon, remove from the heat (the curd thickens further as it cools). Pour into a very clean glass jar or jars and seal very tightly.

Stored in a dry, dark place, the curd should keep for at least 3 months.

Full of vitamin C and nourishing energy; a delicious alternative to jam or filling for small tartlets.

Apple chutney

INGREDIENTS

2¼lb / 1kg slightly underripe (windfall) apples
1½ cups / ¾lb / 350g sugar
scant cup / 5oz / 150g seedless white grapes or sultanas
1 stick celery, finely chopped
1 small onion, finely chopped
pinch ground ginger
1 clove garlic, crushed or chopped
1 teaspoon coriander seeds
2 hot red (chilli) peppers, crumbled
1 tablespoon mustard powder
1 cup / 8fl oz / 225ml best quality white wine (or cider) vinegar

METHOD

Peel and core the apples; slice into a preserving pan; add the vinegar, chilli peppers and mustard. Cook until just tender; drain off the vinegar before pushing the apples through a sieve or breaking up with a fork. Return to the pan with the vinegar; add the chopped celery and onion and all the other ingredients. Simmer for 10 minutes, stirring frequently. Remove from the heat and leave to stand for 24 hours in a large china mixing bowl.

Unless the chutney is already very thick, simmer for 5-10 minutes more to reduce further; make sure it does not stick and burn. Ladle into jars; allow to cool before sealing tightly.

Many cooks have perfected their own special recipe for apple chutney, to go with curries, cold meat and poultry.

Quince cheese

INGREDIENTS

2¼lb / 1kg quinces
5¾ cups / 2lb 14oz / 1.3kg sugar
2 lemons
½ cup / 4fl oz / 125ml water

METHOD

Peel and core the quinces, dropping them into a bowl full of cold acidulated water (using the juice of 1½ lemons) to prevent them turning brown. When they are all ready, drain and place in a preserving pan with the water and the juice of the remaining half lemon, together with a piece of peel.

Bring slowly to the boil and cook gently while stirring until tender. Sieve the quinces, return to the pan, add 4½ cups / 2¼lb / 1kg of the sugar and bring to a gentle boil, skimming when necessary and stirring, until the mixture reaches the correct consistency for jam and looks very smooth and homogeneous.

Pour into small moulds or shapes while still hot, or spread out on a marble slab or in shallow trays which have been sprinkled with superfine/caster sugar; when cold, cut the solidified quince "cheese", which should be about ¾in / 1½cm thick, into squares or shapes. Roll in more sugar and keep in airtight tins in a dry cupboard.

Known as "cotognata" in Italy, "membrillo" in Spain, this was once a favourite snack for children: delicious, refreshing and full of vitamins.

Fruit salad

INGREDIENTS

- *8¾lb / 4kg (net weight) mixed fruit: apples, pears, peaches, apricots, gooseberries, cherries, pineapple*
- *1 lemon*
- *2 quarts / 3½ pints / 2 litres water*
- *4½ cups / 2¼lb / 1kg sugar*

METHOD

Peel, trim and pit/stone all the fruit (the variety will change according to season) and slice into small pieces; sprinkle the apples and pears with a little lemon juice to prevent them discolouring and prepare them last.

Mix all the fruit gently and place in jars.

Make a sugar syrup, boiling the water with the sugar for about 2 minutes. Remove from the heat and pour while still hot into the jars containing the fruit salad.

Seal and sterilize for 20 minutes (see page 119). Store in a cool, dark place.

When serving the fruit salad, top each portion with some whipped cream or ice-cream, or try a little mixed berry sauce.

Orange crunch

INGREDIENTS

- *1⅓ cups / 10½oz / 300g sugar*
- *2 cups / 10½ oz / 300g shelled sweet almonds*
- *1 orange*
- *a little oil*

METHOD

Blanch the almonds in boiling water and peel. Spread on a cookie/baking tray and bake for a short while in a moderately hot oven (they must not colour at all); chop coarsely.

Place the sugar in a small copper saucepan (or in a stainless-steel pan), add the strained juice of the orange and melt the sugar with it over a moderate heat. Stir the mixture whenever it shows signs of boiling. Continue cooking over a very low heat, stirring only when absolutely necessary. When the thickened syrup shows signs of colouring a pale golden brown, add the chopped almonds and a teaspoon of the grated orange peel (no pith).

Stir vigorously when you add the nuts and remove from heat as soon as the mixture leaves the sides of the saucepan; turn out on to a lightly oiled marble slab.

Use a lightly oiled spatula to spread the mixture out to a thickness of about ½in / 1cm, preventing it from breaking up by pressing it together.

Leave to cool and then cut into squares or triangles or shape of your choice. Wrap in foil and store in tins or air-tight glass jars in a cool, dry place.

Eat on its own, or crumble over ice-cream sundaes and other desserts, such as vanilla custards.

Preserving vegetables

in oil, vinegar or brine

You can preserve vegetables in their own cooking liquid, in brine, oil or vinegar, and by salting or drying.

Drying is probably the most ancient of all methods and not practised on a large scale nowadays except for such items as wild and cultivated mushrooms, tomatoes, olives, eggplants/aubergines and nearly all culinary herbs. This is partly because commercial drying of vegetables calls for large, well-ventilated premises and special equipment to ensure total dehydration.

Salting in brine means that the vegetables are kept in a salt and water solution and only requires care in measuring the proportion of salt to water.

The age-old practice of preserving in oil or vinegar is very reliable and suits almost all vegetables. Top quality olive oil (first pressing, cold pressed) and excellent red or white wine vinegar (or cider or good, mild malt vinegar) must be used to ensure success. When oil is used, other ingredients are also included such as salt, spices and herbs, and the vegetables are often blanched in vinegar and then drained before being immersed in the oil (the blanching vinegar can be put to good use afterwards).

How to pick and choose vegetables for preserving

The following hints will help to ensure that your preserved vegetables keep well and taste good.

All produce must be in perfect condition and the best you can find, so preserve vegetables when they are in full season, that is when they are most plentiful, or cheapest, and have the fullest taste.

Make sure that the vegetables you pick, or any near them, have not been sprayed with any chemicals or fertilizers recently. There is usually no way of knowing whether vegetables from the shops or wholesalers have been treated with insecticides or pesticides, so they should be washed more thoroughly before processing. You should gather them as soon as they are fully mature (except where the recipe states otherwise), selecting only perfectly sound, succulent produce with no signs of discolouration, cracks or blemishes.

You should gather and preserve the vegetables on the same day whenever possible, so that they are still very fresh.

Preparing the vegetables

Nearly all vegetables have to be lightly cooked or, preferably, just blanched before processing, and it is important not to let the blanching liquid stop boiling if you want the vegetables to keep their colour and texture. They should be plunged into fast boiling water, fully immersed by pressing gently with a wooden spatula and blanched with no lid on. Do not use too much salt or the vegetables will tend to be tough; always use coarse or untreated salt (which, unlike table salt, has no additives to keep it dry and free running).

Follow the blanching times given meticulously: a few moments too long and your vegetables may be almost mushy by the time you come to use them; they should be crisp with plenty of bite left.

Equipment for preparing and preserving vegetables

This depends on your chosen method, be it canning/bottling in the cooking liquid, oil, vinegar, brine or salt. Basically you need:

- a few knives (stainless steel) of varying sizes for peeling and slicing the vegetables
- several long-handled wooden spoons and wooden spatulas for pushing the vegetables down into the blanching liquid and stirring; a couple of ladles
- a colander for draining vegetables
- a fine hair sieve and a vegetable mill (stainless steel) for sieving tomatoes and other produce
- a skimmer or perforated spoon or ladle for removing scum and lifting vegetables out of the boiling blanching liquid
- a measuring jug, with clearly marked volume/capacity for accurate liquid measurement

  assorted stainless-steel pans and saucepans (preferably hollow-ground copper-bottomed)
- a large preserving pan, either copper or stainless steel to ensure good conductivity and an even heat
- a gadget for sealing bottles and a supply of the metal

bottle caps or tops for it to clamp in place
- a fairly large stainless-steel grater for certain types of vegetables which are to be processed in purée form
- a large, solid hardwood chopping block used for vegetables only (wood tends to become scented)
- 2 or 3 large china bowls (or hard plastic or enamelled cast iron)
- one or two large, wide glass or china bowls
- several cotton, canvas or calico cloths
- a steam pressure canner with gauge or a large pressure cooker, with the usual graduated weights for pressure
- plenty of glass jars, small and large, earthenware jars or pots; small wooden boxes for dried vegetables

A few helpful hints before you start

- Wash the vegetables thoroughly but do not leave to soak in water; if you have grown them yourself, or know they come from a clean, chemical-free environment or source, just wipe them with a damp cloth and spread them out to dry.

- Remember to cook each type of vegetable separately when, for instance, you are preserving a mixture or macédoine of vegetables, as each variety needs a different cooking time.

- Add a pinch of sugar when making tomato sauce or purée, to counter the acid taste.

- Try to choose preserving jars which will hold just enough for one meal (the size will vary according to the number of people you have to serve), as canned or bottled vegetables should be used as soon as possible after opening. See that the jars have no nicks or cracks in them. Patent jars, either the screw-collar or clamp type, are best to ensure a totally airtight seal. If you use the screw-collar jars, buy the patent lids which have the rubber rings bonded to their undersides; never use them twice. If using the system which calls for separate rubber rings, these should ideally also be used only once; buy before the preserving season gets fully under way, before the shops run out of supplies, and store as recommended in the fruit section on page 9. Just before using them, you can wash them in a weak solution of baking soda/bicarbonate of soda and water and then rinse well under the cold tap.

- It is also just as well to boil the jars and lids for about 10 minutes before using them; then turn upside down on a clean cloth to dry; do not wipe them dry. To make doubly sure of total cleanliness, a vital concern when preserving vegetables and never more so than when preserving them in their own liquid, which can present problems, you may wish to give the jars a final rinse in a weak solution of water and vinegar or lemon juice, which will act as a mild disinfectant. The inside of the jars and their contents must be a

totally sterile environment: a moment's carelessness could lead to bacteria getting inside the jar and producing mould or even contamination and toxins.
- Do not wash the cloths or filters with detergent of any sort, unless you wash them at high temperatures in a washing machine with several rinses.
- Keep the jars in a dry, dark place, ideally a dry cellar.
- Remember to label your jars before putting them away, showing contents, date of canning/bottling and a "use by" date.
- Check the jars frequently during the first week following canning/bottling, looking out for any signs of deterioration: tiny upward-rising bubbles, cloudiness, oozing or bulging of the lids. If these vegetables were preserved in their cooking liquid, discard without any hesitation whether the contents smell unpleasant or not; if preserved by any other method, check to see whether there is any strange or unpleasant odour; if there is, discard. If not, bring the contents to the boil, simmer briskly (205-210°F / 96-99°C) for 15 minutes before using.
- Once you have put the jars away, try not to move them: changes in temperature and humidity can cause the rubber bands or rings to perish, destroying the seal.
- If you have difficulty in opening a jar, immerse the top in hot water or run hot water over it and then try again; the metal should have expanded, making it easier to open.
- Once the jar has been opened, use it up as soon as possible, keeping any leftover contents in the refrigerator.
- If you are a beginner at canning/bottling, restrict yourself to small batches for the first year; then, if your methods were not up to standard, you will not feel you have a disaster of epic proportions on your hands in terms of wasted time, trouble and money. You will grow more confident as you become more experienced.

Canning/bottling vegetables
When canning or bottling vegetables in their cooking or blanching liquid or in a light brine, you need to be particularly careful; it is vital to sterilize the filled, sealed jars, or use the Tyndall method (see page 120).

Sterilization - The hermetically sealed jars are boiled in water for the time stated in the recipe; you should have a steam pressure gauge sterilizer or, at least, a large pressure cooker which can accommodate your largest jars, several at a time. Cover the bottom of the sterilizer or cooker neatly with a folded sheet of newspaper to prevent any likelihood of breakage when the jars are boiled; to make doubly sure, wrap each jar in newspaper also.

Jars with hot contents are lowered into hot or tepid water and cold ones into cold water and then brought slowly up to the correct temperature/pressure to sterilize for the time stipulated. Allow the jars to cool completely in the water before removing.

Checking the seal - To ensure that the jars are absolutely airtight, unscrew the metal collar of each jar and remove (or release the clamps on the other variety of jar). Holding the whole jar by the glass lid or thick disc alone – above the rubber ring and lip of the jar itself – lift it up above a folded cloth (in case the seal is not satisfactory and the lid and jar part company). If the lid adheres tightly, bearing the whole weight of the jar, all is well. If the lid comes away from the jar at all, you *must* repeat the sterilization process again with each faulty jar, from start to finish. Check first that the fault does not lie with a perished rubber ring, and that the jar is not nicked or cracked.

The Tyndall method - Named after its inventor, James Tyndall, this is a particularly safe and thorough way of killing bacteria in canning/bottling and is often used for fish and meat. It is more lengthy and the process is repeated at least three times, with a 24-hour interval between each processing. Place the jars in water, which must cover the tops of the jars by at least 4in / 10cm in a sterilizer or deep water bath, and boil for 45 minutes at a constant temperature of 212°F / 100°C. Remove from the sterilizer and leave to cool, wrapped in cloths, for 24 hours (they must not cool too quickly). This whole process is repeated twice more, with the 24-hour gap in between each time. Only then can the jars be stored away in a cool, dark place. (The seal must be checked after each boiling, when cooled.) This is a lengthy procedure but extra safe; the first boiling kills off bacteria and toxins present in the foods which are being preserved; any bacteria which were not killed by this processing, and which multiply during the next 24 hours, will be destroyed by the next sterilization. The third sterilization is to ensure there are absolutely no bacteria present which could prove harmful, or even fatal, in foods to be stored for a long time.

NOTE - Vegetables, unlike fruit, do not have a high acid content, and are therefore less resistant to bacteria. If the instructions for sterilizing, given above, are followed meticulously there is no cause for worry. But do check the jars every so often for bulging, leaking or oozing, and look out for cloudiness or mushiness. If in any doubt, discard.

Preserving vegetables in salt, cooking liquid or brine

You need never be at a loss for starters
or snacks when you have unexpected guests:
everything can be at your fingertips
in the store cupboard.
Everyone will love your wholesome
home-made antipasto platters
and unusual vegetables
served with the main course.

Basil and capers preserved in salt

Asparagus in light brine

INGREDIENTS

2¼lb / 1kg asparagus

salt to taste

METHOD

Trim the asparagus spears at the thicker, tough end so that they will fit easily, upright, in jars. Delicately peel the top layer of skin with a very sharp knife, removing such skin as comes off easily. Place in the jars, tips uppermost.

Bring a fairly large pan of salted water to the boil for a minute or two; leave to cool and then pour over the asparagus. Seal the jars tightly, sterilizing for 1 hour if you are using 2lb (approx) / 1kg jars (see page 119).

It is recommended that you use the Tyndall method for this vegetable (see page 120) for safety and success. Store the jars in a cool, dark place.

Wash the asparagus well in plenty of cold water before using; sauté in hot, frothy butter (preferably unsalted), transfer to hot plates and sprinkle liberally with freshly grated Parmesan cheese.

Basil preserved in salt

INGREDIENTS

approx ½lb / 200g fresh basil leaves

sufficient quantity best quality olive oil

½lb / 250g fine salt (untreated, no additives)

METHOD

Pick the basil in the morning, choosing stems which show no signs of starting to flower. Wash them and spread to dry quickly on paper towels, preferably in the open air. Detach the leaves from their stems and place in small, wide-necked jars, in layers alternated with the salt – a handful of basil leaves followed by a tablespoon of salt. The final layer should be a salt layer. Press down gently to expel as much air trapped between the leaves as possible. Trickle a little olive oil over the top layer and seal. Keep in a dry, dark place.

When you cook with these basil leaves (or use them in salads), remember that they are very salty, so go easy on the salt which you would normally use; sometimes no more salt need be added.

Asparagus, peas and celery in light brine

Capers preserved in salt

INGREDIENTS

$4\frac{1}{2}$lb / 2kg capers

$4\frac{1}{2}$lb / 2kg block or coarse salt

METHOD

If you are picking capers from your own garden, choose those which are not yet open and leave $\frac{1}{4}$in / 2mm of stalk attached to them. Wash, drain well and spread on clean cloths in the sun for 2 hours to dry. Layer the salt and capers in jar(s) until full. Seal and keep in a cool, dry place.

Before using, soak in cold water, changing the water several times, and use little or no more salt in the dish to which they are added.

Artichokes in light brine

INGREDIENTS

$4\frac{1}{2}$lb / 2kg medium-sized artichokes

2 lemons

a few bay leaves

a few peppercorns

approx 1 tablespoon coarse salt

METHOD *(see illustrated instructions on pages 192-3)*

Wash and trim the artichokes (they must be young and tender), taking off enough of the outer, harder leaves to expose the paler, tender leaves inside. Snip off the sharp points of the leaves with scissors but leave a little of the stalk attached, scraping off the outer skin with a sharp knife. Work quickly; as each artichoke is completed, plunge into a large bowl of tepid acidulated water (using the juice of both lemons) to prevent the artichokes discolouring. Remove the artichokes from the water, shake off excess moisture and place in jars together with a few peppercorns and a bay leaf in each. Bring enough water to cover all the artichokes in their jars to the boil with the salt (you will need about 1 quart / $1\frac{3}{4}$ pints / 1 litre); when the salt has dissolved, pour over the artichokes.

Seal the jars very tightly and sterilize in the steam-pressure gauge sterilizer or pressure cooker: place the slotted or perforated disc in the bottom, with the raised side downwards; pour in 3 pints / 2 pints 13fl oz / $1\frac{1}{2}$ litres water and place the jars on the smooth, upper surface of the disc. If you are using small jars, you may be able to arrange them in two layers, inserting another disc between the two. Place the lid on top and make sure it is tightly engaged (drawing it from right to left in the usual way when locking the pressure cooker lid into place). Set the temperature gauge to 248°F/120°C and place the pressure cooker on the heat. Bring to the boil and then simmer for 10 minutes. Turn off the heat without lifting or releasing the pressure valve; when the pressure gauge shows it is safe to open the cooker, remove the lid. Leave the jars to cool and then put away in a cool, dark storeroom or cupboard.

Prepare the artichokes for eating by rinsing in plenty of cold water, and then drain; dress with olive oil and lemon juice.

Carrots in light brine

INGREDIENTS

4½lb / 2kg small, sweet tender carrots
a few pinches sugar
salt to taste

METHOD

Scrub the carrots and cut lengthwise in half; if they are very long, cut each length in half. Blanch in boiling salted water for 10-15 minutes; drain and leave to cool. Place in jars and cover with a fresh quantity of boiled, salted water which has been allowed to cool completely. Add a pinch of sugar to each jar, seal and sterilize for 1½ hours (see method on page 119).

You can serve these carrots as they are, drained and dressed with oil, lemon, pepper and salt, warmed through first if wished by plunging into boiling water for a few seconds; or sauté them in a mixture of oil and butter, adding plenty of finely chopped parsley. You can use them in the traditional way, for example with roast meats, or they can be added to home-made soups, such as minestrone.

Sauerkraut

INGREDIENTS

4½lb / 2kg white cabbage
a few juniper berries
a few seeds caraway or fennel (optional)
a few sprigs tarragon
a few bay leaves
1 sprig basil
pinch thyme
generous 1¼ cups / 10½oz / 300g salt
a few peppercorns

METHOD

Shred the cabbage finely with a very sharp knife. Place in a large earthenware or china bowl and add a little salt, the juniper berries, caraway or fennel, peppercorns and the herbs. Mix well and leave to stand for 30 minutes. Pack into earthenware jars or pitchers, or a small wooden barrel, alternating each layer with a layer of salt. Cover with a few reserved whole leaves of cabbage (sound and undamaged); place a linen cloth over these and then press, using a wooden disc or earthenware plate which will just fit inside the barrel or jar; place a weight on top to press the sauerkraut down well (the salty juice should come just above the wooden disc or plate). Leave to ferment in a cool place; the sauerkraut should be ready after about 50 days.

During this time, skim off the greyish liquid from the top of the cabbage with a skimmer or shallow ladle at frequent intervals.

You can eat the sauerkraut after 2 months; after removing some from the container, wipe round the edges with a clean cloth and clean the wooden disc. Serve raw or cooked.

Gherkins in brine

INGREDIENTS

6½lb / 3kg small, pickling cucumbers
1 lemon (peel only)
a few leaves basil and tarragon
a few peppercorns
½ cup / 4oz / 120g sugar
2 bay leaves
1-1¼ cups / ½lb / 240g coarse salt
generous 1lb / 500g fine salt

METHOD

Wash and dry the cucumbers. Pack into an earthenware jar in layers, alternating with the fine salt and small pieces of lemon peel. Cover and leave to stand for 24 hours. The next day, drain all the liquid from the cucumbers and spread on a clean cloth to dry in the sun or in a well-ventilated place.

When they are dry, pack into the same earthenware jar(s), distributing the basil and tarragon leaves and the peppercorns evenly amongst them.

When the jars are filled to within about 1½in / 4cm of the top, make the brine: boil 3 quarts / 5¼ pints / 3 litres water briefly with the coarse salt, the sugar and the bay leaves. Leave to cool and then cover the cucumbers with it. Keep the cucumbers submerged by inserting a wooden or plastic disc which will just fit inside the neck of the jar. Seal and keep cool and dark. A greyish liquid will rise to the top as time goes by: this is normal and in no way means that the gherkins are contaminated.

Rinse briefly before eating.

Green/French beans in light brine

INGREDIENTS

4½lb / 2kg green / French beans
salt to taste

METHOD

Top and tail the beans. Bring a large pan of water to the boil and plunge the beans into it. Add salt and boil fast for 2 minutes. Drain and spread out to let them dry and cool. Place in jars and cover with the salted water in which they were boiled, which should be kept hot while the beans are draining and cooling. Seal tightly and sterilize for 15-20 minutes (see page 119). Keep in a cool, dark place.

When you want to use the beans, drain thoroughly, rinse in cold running water and sauté in butter, or simmer for a few minutes in a home-made savoury tomato sauce.

Artichokes in light brine

Button mushrooms preserved in salt

INGREDIENTS

- *2¼lb / 1kg tiny button mushrooms or wild Armillaria mellea*
- *2¼lb / 1kg coarse salt*

METHOD

Trim off any earthy tips of the stem, rinse briefly in cold water and add to fast boiling water. As soon as the water returns to the boil, drain and spread on clean cloths to dry for 3-4 days.

Place a layer of salt just under ¼in / about ½cm thick in the jar (or jars), cover with a layer of mushrooms and continue layering until all the mushrooms and salt are used. Finish with a layer of salt.

Seal the jar(s) and store in a cool, dark place.

When the time comes to cook with these mushrooms, take them out of the salt, rinse and then leave to soak in plenty of cold water for 24 hours. Drain, dry and sauté in abundant hot olive oil, with a little garlic if liked. Otherwise you can cook them with finely chopped garlic and parsley and add fresh or home-made tomato sauce.

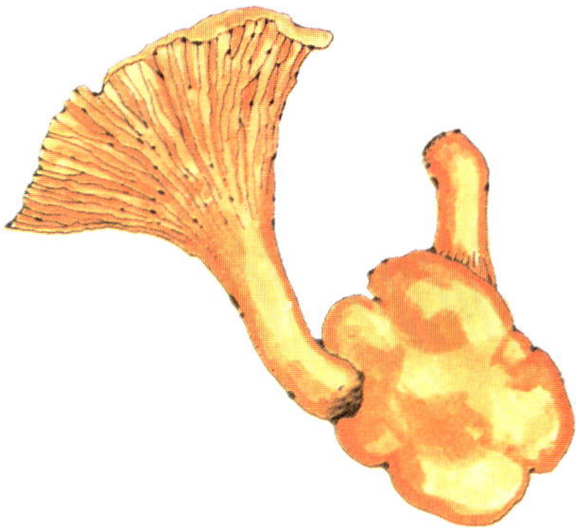

Chanterelle mushrooms in spiced brine

INGREDIENTS

- *2¼lb / 1kg chanterelles (Cantharellus cibarius)*
- *a few peppercorns*
- *2 cloves*
- *small piece cinnamon bark*
- *3/2 basil leaves*
- *1 bay leaf*
- *salt to taste*

METHOD

Check the mushrooms, trimming where necessary, and wash quickly under cold running water. If you have any large mushrooms, cut in two so they are all roughly the same size. Bring plenty of salted water to the boil and plunge the mushrooms into it, leaving them in the water for only a second or two once it has returned to the boil. Drain and spread out to dry on clean cloths in the sun for 1 hour. Pack into jars, pressing down gently.

Bring 1 quart / 1¾ pints / 1 litre water to the boil with a little salt, the peppercorns, cloves, cinnamon, the basil leaves and bay leaf. Boil for 2 minutes, then remove from the heat and strain, pouring into the jars to cover the mushrooms completely while still very hot. Seal the jars and sterilize for three-quarters of an hour (see page 119). Keep in a cool, dark place.

When using, drain off the liquid and sauté in oil with chopped garlic and parsley, or simply heat with cooking cream (crème fraîche) and a few flakes of unsalted butter.

Wild mushrooms in spiced brine

INGREDIENTS

4½lb / 2kg edible Boletus or Caesar's Amanita or other edible wild or cultivated mushrooms
a few cloves
2 lemons
a few bay leaves
a few peppercorns
salt to taste

METHOD

Choose evenly sized mushrooms, or cut the larger ones in half or quarters. Discard the stalk ends, check and, if necessary, wash very briefly in cold water.

Bring a large pan of salted water to the boil with some of the peppercorns, the cloves, the juice of the lemons and two pieces of peel. Add the mushrooms, keeping them at a brisk simmer for 5-6 minutes. Drain and leave to cool; when cold, pack into jars.

Bring some fresh water, with salt added, to the boil; allow to cool completely and then pour into the jars to cover the mushrooms. Place a bay leaf or two and a few peppercorns in each jar. Seal tightly and sterilize for 1 hour (see page 119). Put away in a cool, dry, dark place.

Serve as a starter, sprinkled with a little top quality olive oil, or slice and add to rice salads.

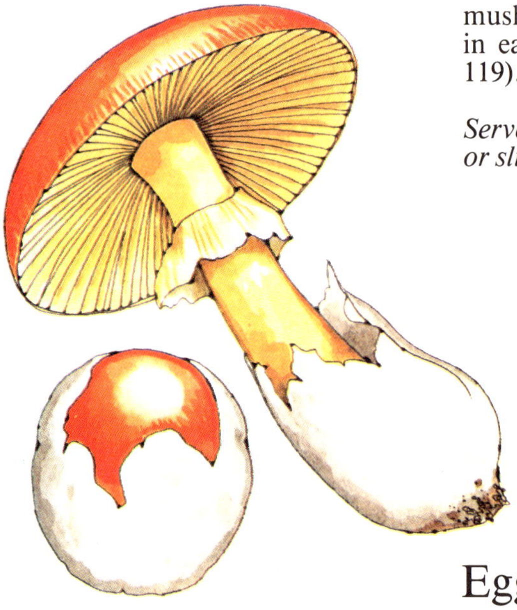

Eggplants/aubergines with basil

INGREDIENTS

8¾lb / 4kg eggplants/aubergines
5-6 basil leaves
1 cup / 7oz / 200g coarse salt
1 tablespoon freshly ground pepper

METHOD

Wipe the eggplants/aubergines with a damp cloth; cut in half and remove the central part if the seeds are easily discernible. Cut into small dice. Mix in a bowl with the salt, pepper and the basil leaves, and then leave to drain in a colander to release their bitter juice for about 5 hours. When the vegetables have released a great deal of liquid, pack quite tightly (with the basil leaves and pepper) into the jars to within ½in / 1cm of the top. Place a waxed paper disc on top. Seal tightly and sterilize for 45 minutes, or use the Tyndall method (see pages 119 and 120).

These eggplants/aubergines can be served as a starter or as a vegetable with a main course. For the former, dress with olive oil and lemon juice; for the latter, sauté with oil, butter, a chopped clove of garlic and plenty of chopped parsley.

Spiced, salted eggplants/aubergines

INGREDIENTS

11lb / 5kg eggplants/aubergines
6-7 cloves garlic
10 hot red (chilli) peppers
20 small, tender basil leaves
1 teaspoon oregano
salt to taste

METHOD

Cut off the stalk and calyx of the eggplants/aubergines and wipe with a damp cloth. Slice lengthwise: the pieces should be about ¼in / ½cm thick. Bring plenty of salted water to the boil and blanch the eggplant/aubergine slices a few at a time, keeping the water at a continuous boil. After each batch has boiled for a minute or two, remove with a slotted spoon, spread out in layers in a colander or large sieve covered by a plate and weight, and drain for 24 hours.

The next day, arrange the vegetables in layers in jars, sprinkling each layer with salt, a few slices of garlic, some pieces of chilli pepper, a few basil leaves and a pinch of oregano. The last layer should be of salt. Place a wooden or plastic disc on top of this, cut to fit snugly inside the top or neck of the jar; place a weight on top of this. As time goes by, the eggplants/aubergines will release more moisture which will rise to the top, over the disc – this can be sponged away or absorbed with a paper towel.

These are usually served as a starter or appetizer with plenty of olive or walnut oil.

Olives in brine

INGREDIENTS

generous 6½lb / 3kg sound olives, not too ripe
a few cloves
1 lemon (peel only, without the pith)
1 teaspoon fennel seeds
1½ cups / 10-11oz / 280-300g salt

METHOD

Place the olives (do not pit/stone) in a large bowl of cold water. Leave to soak for a couple of days, changing the water frequently: this gets rid of the slightly bitter taste. Drain, dry in a large, clean cloth and pack into jars. Bring 3 quarts / 5¼ pints / 3 litres water to the boil with the salt, and pour over the olives when cool. Add the cloves, lemon peel and the fennel seeds, distributing them evenly between the jars. Seal the jars tightly and keep well away from light.

When you want to use the olives, rinse briefly in cold water, drain and serve as part of a mixed antipasto platter, dressed with olive oil, a few tiny strips of lemon or orange peel or a small bay leaf.

Sweet (bell) peppers in brine

INGREDIENTS

desired quantity sound, fleshy sweet (bell) peppers (Asti, Carmagnola and Spanish varieties are good)
sufficient quantity good quality red or white wine vinegar
a sufficient quantity bay leaves
a sufficient quantity cloves
1 large sprig basil leaves
coarse (block) salt to taste

METHOD

Wash the peppers, dry, cut into quarters, removing the stalk and surround, seeds, and membrane. Spread them out on a clean cloth to dry in the sun for about 5 hours. Make a brine while they are drying: for each quart 1¾ pints / 1 litre water allow 1 pint / 18fl oz / ½ litre vinegar, scant ½ cup / 3oz / 80 g coarse salt, 2 bay leaves and 5-6 cloves; boil for 2 minutes and then leave to cool. Place the peppers in the jars with a few basil leaves, making sure there is enough room for the brine to come about 1½in / 3-4cm above the level of the peppers, and about ½in / 1cm from the top of the jar. Seal the jars tightly and keep in a dry, dark, well-ventilated place.

Check the jars every now and then to see that the peppers are still completely covered by the brine, especially if you use earthenware jars which tend to absorb the liquid.

Peas in light brine

INGREDIENTS

4½lb / 2kg hulled/shelled, fresh peas
1 tablespoon / ½oz / 16g sugar
¼ cup / 1½oz / 40g salt

METHOD

When you hull/shell the peas, set aside any very small ones for other uses; the peas for canning/bottling should be of fairly uniform size. Have plenty of lightly salted water boiling fast and pour the peas into it; boil for 3 minutes and then drain. Spread out to dry on clean cloths for a while and then transfer to jars.

Prepare the brine: for this quantity of peas you will need 2 quarts / 3½ pints / 2 litres water and the given quantity of salt and sugar (multiply these quantities if you can/bottle greater quantities). Boil for 2 minutes, then leave to cool and place the peas in the jars. Pour the cold brine on to the peas. Seal tightly and sterilize for 10-15 minutes (see page 119). Remember to check that the seal is perfect after this; if it is not, seal again and repeat the sterilization process.

Try to use a copper or stainless steel preserving pan or large saucepan when preserving peas or any other type of vegetable with this brine method.

Mushrooms in oil

Tomatoes preserved whole

INGREDIENTS

desired quantity oval or egg-shaped sauce tomatoes, (St. Marzano or Flask are good; try to choose acid varieties — see note below)
sufficient quantity basil leaves
salt to taste
pepper to taste

METHOD

Remove the remains of the stalk and calyx from the tomatoes, blanch in boiling water for a few seconds (not more than 30 seconds), then plunge immediately into cold water. Peel the tomatoes with your fingers and place them in a large non-metallic bowl, breaking them up a little. Mix with a little salt, freshly ground pepper and basil leaves, then leave to stand for 30 minutes. Use a slotted or perforated spoon to transfer the tomatoes into jars, leaving behind most of the liquid they have released. Press down gently. Seal tightly and sterilize for 20-30 minutes for a 2lb / 1kg jar (see page 119). Keep the jars in a cool, dark place.

When the tomatoes are needed (say, for a delicious sauce for pasta), sauté chopped onion and garlic in oil, add some or all the tomatoes and a pinch of sugar to lessen the acidity, and simmer. In the USA, and to a lesser extent in the UK, there is a tendency to grow tomatoes which are less acidic; this can present problems for preserving. Try to use only the older, more acidic varieties.

Tomato sauce

INGREDIENTS

11lb / 5kg tomatoes
2 onions
½ cup / 4fl oz / 125ml olive oil
a few fresh basil leaves
¼ cup / 2oz / 50g sugar
salt to taste
pepper to taste

METHOD

Wash the tomatoes briefly in cold water. Slice off the stalk end and discard. Squeeze the tomatoes to get rid of the excess juice and the seeds. Put the tomatoes through a meat grinder/mincer using the largest gauge disc (or through a very coarse mesh/perforation food mill) without removing the skins. Sauté the chopped onion in the oil. Add the puréed tomatoes, the salt and the freshly ground pepper to taste. Cook for about 10 minutes, stirring and removing any scum or froth. Add a few basil leaves and a pinch of sugar. Pour the hot sauce into jars, seal tightly and sterilize for 20 minutes (see page 119). Put away in a cool, dark, well-ventilated storage space.

If you wish, you can add extra flavour to the sauce while it is simmering, with a chopped mixture of parsley, sage, rosemary and oregano.

Tomato paste/purée

INGREDIENTS

11lb / 5kg sound, ripe tomatoes
olive oil as required
3-4 bay leaves
¼ cup / 2oz / 50g sugar
2oz / 50g freshly ground pepper
pinch salt

METHOD

Slice off the stalk end of each tomato and discard; squeeze to get rid of the seeds and excess juice. Place in a large non-metal pan with the bay leaves, salt, pepper and the sugar. Bring to the boil and then simmer, stirring and skimming when necessary. Cook for 15 minutes, remove from the heat and put through a food mill or sieve. Return to the pan and bring back to the boil, stirring continuously as the purée will thicken considerably and tend to stick and burn. It should be very thick indeed. Taste and add more salt if necessary. Remove from the heat and pour into jars, placing a disc of waxed paper or a thin layer of olive oil on the surface of each jarful of paste/purée. Seal the jars and sterilize for 20 minutes (see page 119). Store in a cool, dark, well-ventilated place.

If you add 1 generous pinch / 1g salicylic acid for every 2¼lb/ 1 kg paste/purée, there is no need to sterilize.

Tomato juice

INGREDIENTS

sound, very ripe tomatoes

METHOD

Wash the tomatoes and then push through a hair (non-metallic) sieve. Pour the resulting juice into coloured glass bottles (dark brown or green) which must be scrupulously clean and absolutely dry. Seal the bottles (preferably using a patent bottle-top sealer) and sterilize for 20-25 minutes (see page 119). Store in a cool place. Make the tomato juice the day you pick the tomatoes, and preferably not more than an hour or so afterwards. The bottling should take place immediately after sieving the tomatoes, as they will ferment if not processed at once. If you like, add a little brandy or vodka or lemon juice and sugar to your juice once sieved, allowing for each 2¼lb / 1kg juice about ¼ cup / 2fl oz / 50ml brandy or vodka, or the juice of 2 juicy lemons and ¼ cup / 2oz / 50g sugar. Or just add sugar (¾ cup / 5oz / 150g for 2¼lb / 1kg juice).

A refreshing apéritif in the hot summer months.

Tomatoes preserved whole and Tomato sauce

Leeks in light brine

INGREDIENTS

4½lb / 2kg cleaned leeks, white part only
10 peppercorns
2-3 bay leaves
salt to taste
2-3 tablespoons olive oil

METHOD

Wash the leeks thoroughly and slice crosswise into 1½-2in / 4-5cm lengths.

Boil the leeks in plenty of salted water for 8-10 minutes, together with the peppercorns and the bay leaves.

Transfer the leeks from the pan to preserving jars, using a slotted or perforated spoon, and press down gently. Remove and discard the peppercorns and bay leaves. Add just enough of the cooking liquid to cover. Dribble a little oil on to the surface of the water. Seal tightly. Sterilize for 45 minutes, or use the Tyndall method (see pages 119 and 120). Store in a cool, dark place.

When it is time to use the leeks, drain off as much liquid as possible and then cook according to your chosen recipe (buttered, with cream, or coated with béchamel sauce and browned in the oven).

Scorzonera/salsify in light brine

INGREDIENTS

4½lb / 2kg black scorzonera/salsify
1-1½ tablespoons all-purpose plain white flour
1 lemon
salt to taste

METHOD

Use a potato peeler to peel the scorzonera/salsify. Slice into 1½-2in / 4-5cm lengths; cut any large pieces in half to ensure even cooking. As you peel the salsify, drop the pieces into a bowl of water, to which nearly all the lemon juice and the flour has been added, to avoid discolouration. Boil in plenty of salted water for about 1 hour.

Drain, place in jars and cover with the cooking liquid, acidulated with a few drops of lemon juice (or boil fresh water, lightly salted and acidulated, and use to cover). Seal jars and sterilize for 30 minutes (see page 119 for method).

When it is time to use the scorzonera/salsify, drain well. Sauté 1-2 cloves garlic in olive oil to flavour; add the salsify and plenty of finely chopped parsley and heat through.

Celery in light brine

INGREDIENTS

4½lb / 2kg celery
1 lemon
salt to taste
freshly ground pepper to taste

METHOD

Choose crisp tender bunches of celery and try to select those which have a good heart. Cut the stalks to lengths which will fit in the jars and cut the heart in quarters. Place in a bowl and leave under a running cold tap. Meanwhile, boil plenty of salted water which has been lightly acidulated with the juice of the lemon. Plunge the drained celery into it and boil for 2-3 minutes; remove from the water and place on a tilted chopping board to drain. Bring a pan of fresh, lightly salted water to the boil for 2 minutes and leave to cool. When the blanched celery is completely cold, arrange upright in the jars. Pour in enough of the cold salted water to cover. Place a few peppercorns in each jar and add a few drops of lemon juice. Seal the jars tightly and sterilize for about 30 minutes in water (see page 119). When cold, store in a cool, dark place.

Invaluable when making minestrone and other soups, or for fricassees and braised dishes. The best celery for canning /bottling has large, fleshy stalks which are green or white and very tender. Do not use the types which tend to have almost hollow stalks.

Salted mixed soup vegetables

INGREDIENTS

4½lb / 2kg net weight mixed vegetables (celery, carrots, leeks, zucchini/courgettes, savoy cabbage, etc.
3½oz / 100g coarse salt

METHOD

Wash and trim all the vegetables (add any others which are suitable for minestrone). Drain and dry. Cut into small dice or slices, add the salt and stir. Pack tightly into a jar, cover the top of the vegetables with a wooden or plastic disc which fits snugly into the neck of the jar, and cover with a very clean cloth. Seal and store in a dark, well-ventilated place.

When you want to use the vegetables for the minestrone, soak them in a large bowl of cold water for 24 hours, changing the water as often as necessary for the vegetables to become less salty. Otherwise they can just be rinsed briefly in cold water and added to the unsalted basic bouillon or broth.

These vegetables can also be incorporated in pot roasts and braised dishes.

Vegetables preserved in oil

These preparations are usually served
as classic hors d'oeuvres,
but only a little flair
and imagination are required to put them to other,
lesser known uses as cocktail party snacks
or mouth-watering additions to mixed salads.

Baby artichokes and Aubergines in oil

Garlic in oil

INGREDIENTS

- *30 fat, sound, firm cloves of garlic*
- *sufficient quantity (top quality) olive oil*

METHOD

Remove the thin papery skin covering the garlic cloves and chop them finely, using a sharp knife or two-handled mezzaluna. Place the coarse paste in a clean, dry jar. Pour in enough top quality olive oil to come ¾in / 2cm over the garlic.

Stir with a wooden spoon, seal the jar and keep in a cool, dark place.

If you want to use the flavoured oil rather than the garlic, remember to top the jar with fresh oil so that the garlic remains covered.

This extremely simple preparation provides you with two products: the delicately flavoured oil (if a very subtle hint of garlic is required) and the garlic itself.

Baby artichokes in oil

INGREDIENTS

- *2¼lb / 1kg baby artichokes (Tuscan Violet or other very tender varieties)*
- *1 quart / 1¾ pints / 1 litre white wine or white vinegar*
- *a few bay leaves*
- *1 lemon*
- *1-2 cloves*
- *sufficient quantity olive oil (top quality)*
- *salt to taste*
- *a few peppercorns*

METHOD

Remove and discard the outer, tougher leaves, exposing the paler tender leaves inside.

Trim off the sharp tips of the remaining leaves and trim the stalk to within about ½in / 1cm of the artichoke; use a knife to pull away the strings surrounding the remainder of the stalk, in the same way as you would remove strings of celery. As soon as each artichoke is ready, plunge into plenty of cold water acidulated with the juice of the lemon. Cut the large artichokes in half (even these should be much smaller than the mature artichokes usually seen in the shops). Bring 1 quart / 1¾ pints / 1 litre water to the boil with the wine or vinegar, peppercorns, about 1 teaspoon of salt and the bay leaves. As soon as it has reached a fast boil, add the artichokes, bring back to the boil and then turn down the heat and simmer gently for about 5 minutes.

Drain the artichokes and leave to dry, up-ended, in a colander lined with a clean cloth. Place the artichokes in jars, add a few more peppercorns and a bay leaf to each jar, and cover with oil so the artichokes are completely immersed. Keep cool.

Check the oil level for the next couple of days, adding a little more if necessary.

Cauliflower in oil

INGREDIENTS

approx 7-8½lb / 3-4kg sound, clean cauliflowers
3-4 sprigs tarragon
2-3 bay leaves
small piece cinnamon bark
1 lemon (peel only)
1½ quarts / 2 pints 13fl oz / 1½ litres wine vinegar
cup / 9fl oz / 250ml white wine
sufficient quantity olive oil
10 peppercorns
salte to taste

METHOD *(see illustrated instructions on page 194)*

Cut the leaves and base off the cauliflower and divide into florets of equal size. Soak in a bowl or basin full of heavily salted water. Pour the vinegar and white wine into a large pan and add a few peppercorns, a small piece of cinnamon and lemon peel, the bay leaves and a little salt.

When the mixture has come to a fast boil, add the cauliflower and boil for 5 minutes. Drain well, leave to cool completely and pat gently with paper towels or cloths to absorb any moisture. Place in jars together with a few more peppercorns, pour in sufficient olive oil to cover completely and slip in a sprig of tarragon. Give the oil time to settle, tapping the base of the jar on a cloth gently to eliminate any air pockets. Top up with more oil if necessary and then seal.

Use as hors d'oeuvres or to garnish mixed or rice salads.

Gherkins in oil

INGREDIENTS

generous 6½lb / 3kg gherkins or small pickling cucumbers
1½lb / 700g coarse salt
2 quarts / 3½ pints / 2 litres best wine vinegar
generous cup / 9fl oz / 250ml white wine
4 bay leaves
15 each tarragon and basil leaves (fresh)
4 garlic cloves
10 small pickling (baby) onions
2-3 dried hot red (chilli) peppers
sufficient quantity olive oil

METHOD

Wipe the cucumbers with a damp cloth and place in a large earthenware or glass jar, mixing them with the salt. Leave to stand in a cool place for 24 hours, stirring and turning them from time to time with a wooden spoon. Drain all the liquid they release, bundle them up in a large, clean cloth and hang up to dry for 2-3 hours; return them to the jar(s) together with the bay leaves, basil, tarragon, garlic, coarsely crumbled chilli peppers and baby onions, all mixed together.

Boil the vinegar with the white wine for a moment or two and then pour straight over the contents of the jar(s) to cover completely. When cold, seal the jars and leave to mature for about 10 days, after which the vinegar must be drained (leave all the herbs etc. in the jar) and replaced with good olive oil. Seal the jars again and store in a dry, dark place.

These make a wonderful hors d'oeuvre or starter; good for garnishes too.

Pickled onions in oil

INGREDIENTS

4½lb / 2kg skinned pickling (baby) onions

1 quart / 1¾ pints / 1 litre wine or good malt vinegar

cup / 9fl oz / 250ml white wine

a sufficient quantity olive oil

5-6 cloves

5-6 peppercorns

small piece cinnamon bark

2 bay leaves

¼ cup / 2oz / 50g sugar

salt to taste

METHOD

Place the prepared onions in a large, stainless-steel or enamelled pan, cover with the vinegar and white wine, then add the cloves, cinnamon, sugar, bay leaf and a generous pinch of salt.

Bring to the boil and simmer very gently for 10 minutes. Drain off the vinegar mixture and spread the onions out on clean cloths to dry for about 2 hours. Place the onions in jars with the peppercorns and cover completely with the olive oil. Seal the jars very tightly and store in a dry, dark place.

You may need a couple of practice runs at these onions, making a half batch the first time: if the onions are cooked for too long (if they are on the small side) or not long enough (if they are rather large) they can ferment, even when immersed in oil.

Try to buy pickling onions which are as close to ⅝in / 15mm in diameter as possible and fairly uniform in size.

Piquant button mushrooms in oil

INGREDIENTS

2¼lb / 1kg trimmed, clean button mushrooms

generous 1½ cups / 14fl oz / 400ml olive oil

3-4 dried, hot red (chilli) peppers

4 cloves garlic

1 tablespoon finely chopped parsley (preferably flat-leaved variety)

1 basil leaf

1 lemon

salt to taste

METHOD

Place the prepared mushrooms in a large bowl of acidulated cold water (using the juice of the lemon); if some are rather large, cut in half before adding to the acidulated water. Drain well and spread out on cloths to dry thoroughly, patting them with another clean cloth.

Heat the oil in a large pan, add the garlic cloves (squashed with the flat of a knife blade, not crushed); when the garlic cloves have coloured lightly, remove and discard. Add the mushrooms. Stir well, over a higher heat so they cook quickly. Mix while cooking for 5 minutes. When all the moisture has evaporated add the crumbled chilli peppers, chopped parsley, basil leaf and a generous pinch of salt. Stir well, remove from the heat and tip straight into a jar with all the oil. Seal tightly and sterilize for 10-15 minutes (see page 119). Keep in a cool, dark place.

Serve as an extra vegetable. Use this method for other mushrooms: chanterelles, small Boletus and morels.

Mushrooms in oil with basil

INGREDIENTS

4½lb / 2kg fresh, young cultivated mushrooms

1lb / 500g hot peppers (Jalopeño chilli or cayenne peppers or the milder varieties)

a few leaves fresh basil

sufficient quantity good quality olive oil

sufficient quantity good vinegar

a few bay leaves

1 lemon

1 tablespoon all-purpose/ plain white flour

salt to taste

METHOD

Trim the mushrooms and clean if necessary; cut the larger ones in half. Mix the flour into a large bowl of cold water, add the lemon juice and then the mushrooms.

Pour plenty of vinegar into a stainless-steel or enamelled pan, add 1-2 pinches salt, a couple of bay leaves and bring to a fast boil; add the mushrooms (thoroughly drained). Reduce the heat and simmer for about 10 minutes, drain well and spread to dry on cloths in a well-ventilated place.

Wash the hot red peppers in cold water, remove the stalk and surrounds and then the seeds and membranes inside; rinse again before adding to the boiling vinegar used to cook the mushrooms; cook for 10 minutes and then remove and leave to dry for a few hours. When both the mushrooms and peppers are dry, place in jars together with the basil leaves; pour in the oil in stages as you fill the jars; finish with sufficient oil to cover the mushrooms and peppers. Seal and keep in a cool, dark place.

A good addition to an antipasto selection or as an extra vegetable with a main course.

Boletus mushrooms in oil

INGREDIENTS

4½lb / 2kg Boletus edulis wild mushrooms (commonly known as porcini or cèpes) or other wild edible or cultivated varieties

2-3 cloves

2-3 bay leaves

sufficient quantity olive oil

a few peppercorns

white wine vinegar as required

salt to taste

METHOD

Do not wash the mushrooms unless unavoidable; wipe with a damp cloth. Try to choose small, firm specimens of equal size.

Bring sufficient vinegar to cover all the mushrooms to the boil in a pan with a little salt; add the mushrooms and simmer fast for 2-3 minutes.

Remove from the heat and take the mushrooms out with a slotted spoon or ladle. Drain well before placing in jars with a few peppercorns, a clove, and a few pieces of bay leaf. Pour in enough oil to completely cover the mushrooms and seal the jars.

If the oil sinks below the level of the mushrooms after a few days, add more oil.

Keep in cool, dry and dark storage.

Delicious as one of a selection of hors d'oeuvres or as an embellishment to mixed salads.

Eggplants/aubergines in oil

INGREDIENTS

- *2¼lb / 1kg eggplants/aubergines*
- *a few basil leaves*
- *2-4 garlic cloves*
- *sufficient quantity olive oil*
- *sufficient quantity good quality vinegar*
- *salt to taste*
- *freshly ground pepper to taste*

METHOD

The best eggplants/aubergines to choose for this recipe are the elongated, dark-purple or violet Naples variety or the long slender Japanese type. Rinse briefly in cold water and dry. Slice off the stem and calyx and cut into slices about ¼in / ½cm thick. Sprinkle with plenty of salt and freshly ground pepper before spreading in a single layer in a large sieve or on a tilted plate to drain overnight.

The next day, drain off the liquid and then add the eggplant/aubergine slices to a stainless-steel pan of boiling vinegar; blanch for a few seconds and then remove and spread out to dry in a large sieve or on cloths. Alternate layers of these slices in jar(s) with basil leaves, slivers of garlic and olive oil; top up with more oil to cover. Seal the jar(s) tightly and keep in dry, cool, dark storage.

The eggplants/aubergines will not keep unless immersed in oil, so check the level of the oil fairly frequently.

Olives in oil, Andalusian style

INGREDIENTS

- *2¼lb / 1kg pitted/stoned olives, preserved in brine*
- *scant ¼lb / 100g anchovy fillets, preserved in oil or salt*
- *scant ¼lb / 100g hot red peppers, cleaned and blanched in vinegar (see recipe on page 144)*
- *2 tablespoons / 2oz / 50g salted or pickled capers*
- *scant ½ cup / 3½oz / 100g tuna (in oil)*
- *1 clove garlic*
- *a few bay leaves*
- *1 heaped teaspoon finely chopped parsley and basil*
- *1 heaped teaspoon freshly grated Parmesan cheese*
- *sufficient quantity olive oil (best quality, first pressing)*

METHOD

Buy your olives from shops which sell them out of barrels at competitive prices, choosing the largest ones; pit/stone them if this has not been done; dry in paper towels. Chop all the other ingredients listed, stirring in the Parmesan last of all.

Fill each olive with this mixture (you can use a pastry bag and wide, plain nozzle for speed and convenience, inserting the nozzle in one end and keeping your finger over the other so the mixture is pressed in tightly). Fill the jars, alternating layers of olives with pieces of bay leaf and oil. Top up with oil and cover with a waxed paper disc.

Trickle in more oil, seal tightly and keep in a cool and dark place.

These stuffed olives make a wonderful starter, with or without other hors d'oeuvres, or serve as cocktail snacks, in cold rice salads or just as decoration.

Sweet (bell) peppers in oil and Puglia style peppers

Sweet (bell) peppers in oil

INGREDIENTS

- *4½lb / 2kg sound, fleshy sweet (bell) peppers*
- *sufficient quantity white wine vinegar and white wine*
- *a few bay leaves*
- *a few peppercorns*
- *3-4 cloves garlic (or fewer if wished)*
- *a few leaves basil*
- *sufficient quantity olive oil*
- *salt to taste*

METHOD

Wash the peppers and cut lengthwise in quarters, removing and discarding the stalk and surround, then the seeds and membrane. Spread out in the sun for about 5 hours. Transfer to a stainless steel pan and cover with a mixture of the vinegar and white wine, a pinch of salt, some peppercorns and a bay leaf or two. Bring to the boil and cook for 3-4 minutes. Drain well and spread out in full sunlight to dry about 6-8 hours.

Pack into jars, adding the garlic and basil leaves; pour in enough oil to cover. After a few days, when the oil has been partially absorbed by the peppers, pour in a little more to cover them completely. Seal tightly and store in a cool, dry place.

Serve as part of a starter or with roast meat. Chop finely and add to piquant, savoury sauces.

Parsley in oil

INGREDIENTS

- *fairly large bunch freshly picked parsley*
- *sufficient quantity olive oil*

METHOD

Wash the parsley quickly in cold water and dry completely. Snip into little sprigs and pack into small jars, pressing down gently. Pour in enough oil to cover completely and seal the jars tightly. Store in a dry, dark cupboard.

Use the oil sparingly for salad dressings and on pasta cooked until just tender; it is full of flavour and vitamin C. Basil can be preserved in the same way.

Treviso radish/radicchio rosso in oil

INGREDIENTS

6½lb / 3kg	*Treviso radish/ radicchio rosso or red chicory*
1 quart / 1¾ pints / 1 litre	*wine vinegar*
sufficient quantity	*olive oil*
a few	*peppercorns*
as required	*salt*

METHOD

Trim the radicchio carefully, discarding any damaged or slightly wilted leaves and slicing off the root, but be careful to leave enough base so that the heads remain intact with all the leaves attached; wash in cold water and drain.

Pour the vinegar into a stainless-steel pan and add an equal volume of water; bring to the boil and blanch the radicchio heads, pressing them down into the boiling liquid with a wooden spoon. After a few seconds' blanching, remove with a slotted or perforated spoon, place on a large tilted plate and leave to drain thoroughly; dry in a well-ventilated spot. Place in jars with a few coarsely crushed peppercorns. Press down gently and cover with olive oil. Leave the radicchio to soak in the oil for a couple of days and then cover with more if necessary.

Seal the jars tightly and keep in a cool place.

Provided the radicchio has been very thoroughly dried, there is no need to sterilize the jars. Drain the oil when you need to use the radicchio; best with boiled or poached chicken or turkey.

Zucchini/courgettes in oil

INGREDIENTS

6½lb / 3kg	*zucchini/courgettes (green and white striped or yellow crookneck varieties)*
2 quarts / 3½ pints / 2 litres	*good malt or wine vinegar*
a few	*peppercorns*
a few	*basil leaves*
a few	*bay leaves*
sufficient quantity	*olive oil*
salt	*to taste*

METHOD

Slice off both ends of the zucchini/courgettes and slice diagonally, without peeling, into oblique sections about ½in / 1cm thick. Sprinkle with plenty of salt and spread out on a chopping block, tilted up at one end, to drain for 3-4 hours. When they have released all their excess moisture, bring the vinegar to the boil with the peppercorns, and blanch the zucchini/courgette slices in small batches for 2 minutes, keeping the liquid boiling fast. Drain and spread out to dry on a cloth.

Arrange in layers with a few basil leaves and a couple of bay leaves in each jar. Pour in the oil in stages. Stop when just under 1 in / 2cm from the top of the jar. Add enough oil to cover. Seal and keep in a dry, cool and dark place.

Excellent as a starter, hors d'oeuvre or, chopped, added to uncooked or cooked sauces.

Pickled and marinated vegetables

Easy to make, these very versatile pickles and relishes add a pleasantly sharp note to appetizers, hors d'oeuvres and main dishes of boiled or poached meats and poultry. They can also add the finishing touch to piquant sauces, or you can use them just as they are to garnish cold food and summer salads.

Pickled gherkins

Asparagus in vinegar

INGREDIENTS

generous 6½lb / 3kg sound, fresh asparagus
sufficient quantity good quality white wine vinegar
a few peppercorns
a few sprigs tarragon

METHOD

Wash the asparagus well and cut off the harder, bottom section of the stalk (but for the very tender varieties, snip off just enough stalk to fit into your jars). Tie in bundles, an equal number of spears in each; tie once near the base and again two-thirds up the spears. Bring a large pan full of salted water to the boil; add the asparagus and blanch for 2-3 minutes without the lid on.

Use two forks, hooked into the two pieces of string on each bundle, to lift them carefully out of the water; dry on a cloth spread over the working surface. Place in the jars, tips uppermost.

Bring the vinegar and peppercorns to the boil and pour straight into the jars through a conical strainer. Place a sprig of tarragon in each jar. Seal and keep in a cool place.

If you prefer your asparagus less sharp-tasting, add salted boiling water to the vinegar, using a ratio of 1 to 9.

Pickled beets/beetroot

INGREDIENTS

generous 6½lb / 3kg baby beets/beetroot
2 quarts / 3½ pints / 2 litres good malt or red wine vinegar
a few peppercorns
4-6 juniper berries
2 cloves
small piece cinnamon bark
1 onion
2-3 sticks/stalks celery
selection of herbs (optional)
salt to taste

METHOD

Scrub the beets/beetroot carefully with a fairly soft brush under cold running water; place them in a large pan of cold salted water and bring to the boil, cooking until tender (this will take a long time: allow up to 1 hour even for the tiniest of beets/beetroot). Leave to cool in the cooking liquid, drain, peel and cut into small dice.

Mix 3¼ cups / 1¼ pints / 750ml lightly salted water with the vinegar and all the spices and flavourings; boil for 5 minutes and then leave to cool. Place the beets/beetroot in the jars and pour the strained preserving liquid over them.

Sterilize the jars for 15-20 minutes (see page 119) and keep in a cool, dark and dry place.

For salads, either on their own with sour cream dressing or mixed with other vegetables.

Marinated beets/beetroot

INGREDIENTS

- *4½lb / 2kg baby beets/beetroot*
- *1 quart / 1¾ pints / 1 litre red or white wine vinegar*
- *1-2 bay leaves*
- *a few leaves basil*
- *3/2 tablespoons salt*
- *5 peppercorns*

METHOD

Snip off the leaves of the beets, leaving about ½in / 1cm of stalk attached. Wash and scrub very well under cold running water and then bring to the boil from cold in a large uncovered pan full of water; cook for 1-1½ hours depending on size. (Test by piercing them to the centre with a very sharp pointed knife – it should slide in easily.)

Leave to cool in their cooking liquid, then drain, reserving just over 1 cupfu / 9fl oz / ¼ litre of liquid; leave this to stand to clear a little. Peel the beets and leave in a sieve to drain off any remaining moisture for 5 minutes, then place in jars.

Bring the vinegar briefly to the boil with the reserved cooking liquid and a little salt; add the peppercorns, bay leaves and basil leaves. When cold, pour over the beets, covering them completely. Seal the jars and store in a cool, dark place.

Good when mixed with Russian salad (cut into small dice first). Or use for borscht (hot beetroot soup).

Capers in vinegar

INGREDIENTS

- *2¼lb / 1kg capers*
- *1 quart / 1¾ pints / 1 litre good malt or wine vinegar*
- *a few cloves*
- *1 bay leaf*
- *1 basil leaf*
- *salt to taste*

METHOD

Wash and drain the capers; sprinkle with plenty of salt and leave to stand, in a china or glass bowl, for 2 days.

Bring the vinegar to the boil with the cloves, bay leaf and basil leaf; boil for 2 minutes, then remove from the heat. Transfer the capers to jars, leaving behind most but not all of the salt. Pour in enough of the lukewarm vinegar to cover them and leave to stand until cold. Seal the jars and keep in a cool, dry storeroom.

Rinse in cold water to remove excess salt and vinegar, drain well and sprinkle with oil when serving. A good accompaniment to antipasti or cold meats, it can also be added to sauces (such as caper sauce), or served with boiled mutton or lamb.

Baby artichokes in spiced vinegar

INGREDIENTS

2¼lb / 1kg artichokes (young and tender)
sufficient quantity white wine vinegar
2-3 cloves
2 bay leaves
1 lemon
olive oil as required
a few peppercorns

METHOD

Peel off and discard the outer, tougher leaves, exposing the paler, tender ones below; trim off the pointed tips of the leaves using scissors, and immerse each artichoke in a bowl of water acidulated with the juice of the lemon.

Bring the vinegar to the boil with a few peppercorns, the cloves and the bay leaves. Add the artichokes and boil for 2 or 3 minutes (if they are tiny, a minute will suffice; if on the large side, give them a little longer). Remove from the heat and leave to cool in the vinegar.

Transfer the artichokes and vinegar to a large jar, ensuring that the vinegar covers the artichokes completely. Trickle a layer of oil on to the surface and seal the jar. Store in a cool, dark place.

Serve as a starter, as a garnish for cold dishes or as the finishing touch to a special rice salad. The vinegar from these artichokes can be used in cold dressings or hot piquant or sweet-sour sauces.

Pickled carrots

INGREDIENTS

2¼lb / 1kg fairly young, tender carrots
sufficient quantity wine vinegar or good malt vinegar
a few basil leaves
generous pinch sugar
a few peppercorns

METHOD

Cut the carrots into equal sized shapes (rounds, matchsticks, dice etc.) after peeling or scrubbing. Blanch for 5-6 minutes depending on size – they should still be crisp. Drain and spread to dry. Pack them into jar(s) and pour in enough vinegar to cover. Add a few small basil leaves, some peppercorns and a pinch of sugar. Seal the jar(s) and store away from light in a cool, dark, dry place.

Make these part of your antipasto platter or chop and incorporate in piquant or sweet-sour sauces to be served with boiled or poached meat or poultry. Can be used as part of a Russian salad.

Cauliflower in vinegar

INGREDIENTS

4½lb / 2kg sound fresh cauliflowers
1 lemon
a few bay leaves
sufficient quantity white wine vinegar
salt to taste
a few peppercorns

METHOD

Remove the cauliflowers' green leaves and base and cut off the florets, making each piece about the size of a walnut (some will have to be cut in half). Place in a large bowl of cold water to which about 2 tablespoons of salt have been added and leave for about 2 hours. Bring plenty of lightly salted water to the boil with a few pieces of lemon peel. Add the drained cauliflower and about 2 teaspoons of lemon juice, and blanch for 2-3 minutes, no longer. Drain and spread out to dry.

When they are completely cold, place in jars. Then heat enough vinegar to cover all the cauliflower florets in their jars with the peppercorns, bay leaves and a little salt. As soon as it boils, pour over the cauliflower; cool before sealing and storing.

If you prefer your cauliflower less sharp, add water to the vinegar (1 part water to 9 parts vinegar) when boiling the pickling marinade.

Pickled gherkins

INGREDIENTS

generous 6½lb / 3kg gherkins or small pickling cucumbers
2 quarts / 3½ pints / 2 litres white wine vinegar
a few bay leaves
2 sprigs tarragon
5-6 cloves
a few basil leaves
a few peppercorns
salt to taste

METHOD

Wash and trim the gherkins and place in a large bowl; mix with plenty of coarse salt (allow about 2 tablespoons salt for each 2¼lb / 1kg of gherkins). Leave to stand for a few hours to draw out excess liquid; remove from the salt, drain and place in a clean bowl.

Heat enough vinegar to completely cover the gherkins, adding the peppercorns, bay leaves, cloves and sprigs of tarragon. When it has boiled, pour immediately over the gherkins. Leave to stand for 24 hours, then drain the vinegar into the pan and boil again. Taste the vinegar and add salt if necessary. Pour the boiling vinegar over the gherkins once more and leave to marinate for a further 24 hours, discarding the cloves. Top up with fresh vinegar if necessary. On the third day, place the gherkins and vinegar in the pan and boil until the gherkins are almost tender but still quite crisp. Cool, place in jars and cover with the vinegar.

Cover and keep in a well-ventilated place.

This method is best for the gherkin type of pickling cucumbers, rather than the larger ridge cucumbers.

Pickled onions

INGREDIENTS

4½lb / 2kg small pickling onions
1 quart / 1¾ pints / 1 litre white wine vinegar
scant ½ cup / 3½oz / 100g sugar
a few basil leaves
a few bay leaves
salt to taste
a few peppercorns

METHOD

Peel the onions and blanch in plenty of boiling salted water, to which 2-3 tablespoons vinegar have been added, for 3 minutes. Drain and dry; transfer to jars, pressing them down gently. Mix the vinegar with the sugar, basil and bay leaves, bring to the boil and pour straight over the onions through a conical sieve. Add a few peppercorns to each jar, together with a couple of fresh basil leaves. Seal tightly and put away in a cool, dark storeroom or cellar.

Serve on their own, or as a canapé, with drinks, or with other pickles. They can also be sliced and served with tuna fish in oil.

Green/French beans in vinegar

INGREDIENTS

4½lb / 2kg tender, young green/French beans
sufficient quantity white wine vinegar
a few bay leaves
olive oil as required
salt to taste
a few peppercorns

METHOD

Top and tail the beans; they should not have any strings, but check and remove these if necessary. Bring sufficient vinegar to cover the beans to the boil in a large stainless-steel pan with a little salt; add the beans, boil fast for 2 minutes, then drain and spread out to dry on a clean cloth. Pack into jars (preferably vertically) and pour in enough oil to cover completely. Place a bay leaf and a few peppercorns in each jar. Seal and keep in a cool, dark place.

Serve these as a starter, with other pickled vegetables.

Pickled yellow wax beans

INGREDIENTS

4½lb / 2kg young, sound yellow wax / yellow French or bobby beans
sufficient quantity white wine vinegar
2 garlic cloves
2 bay leaves
a few basil leaves
a few peppercorns
salt to taste

METHOD

Top and tail the beans; string if necessary. See that they are no more than about 2½in / 6cm long; cut the longer ones in half. Bring a large pan of salted water to a fast boil and plunge in the beans, blanching them for 3-4 minutes. Drain, spread out on a cloth to dry and cool.

Arrange in jars, distributing small pieces of garlic and bay leaf here and there among them, together with basil leaves and peppercorns.

Bring sufficient vinegar to cover all the beans in their jars to the boil, remove from the heat and immediately pour into the jars containing the beans. Leave to cool completely before sealing tightly and then store in a cool, dark place.

Choose very sound, unmarked beans, on the firm side.

Button mushrooms in vinegar

INGREDIENTS

- *4½lb / 2kg cultivated mushrooms*
- *1 lemon*
- *1 tablespoon all-purpose/plain white flour*
- *2 bay leaves*
- *3-4 cloves*
- *2 sprigs tarragon*
- *a few small pieces cinnamon bark*
- *a sufficient quantity white wine vinegar*
- *small quantity olive oil*
- *peppercorns as required*
- *salt to taste*

METHOD *(see illustrated instructions on page 195)*

Trim off the ends of the mushroom stalks, wipe the mushrooms with a damp cloth and then drop into a large bowl containing cold water well mixed with all but 1 table-spoon of the juice of the lemon, and the flour. Bring about 1½ pints / 750ml water to the boil with a little salt and the remaining lemon juice, add the mushrooms, stir well and boil fast for 3-4 minutes.

Pour plenty of vinegar (at least 1 quart / 1¾ pints / 1 litre) into a stainless-steel pan with the cinnamon, cloves, bay leaves and a few pinches of salt; boil for 1 minute.

Drain the mushrooms, spread out to dry on a cloth, then put into one or more jars; pour in enough vinegar to completely cover through a conical sieve. Add a few peppercorns and the tarragon before trickling a thin film of oil over the surface of the vinegar. Seal tightly and store in a dry, dark, well-ventilated place.

If you do not like the flavour of cinnamon with mushrooms, substitute slivers of garlic and small pieces of hot red (chilli) peppers.

Marinated Boletus mushrooms

INGREDIENTS

- *4½lb / 2kg small Boletus mushrooms (porcini, cèpes) or chanterelles or cultivated mushrooms*
- *2 lemons*
- *2 quarts / 3½ pints / 2 litres white wine vinegar*
- *dry white wine if required*
- *a few tablespoons all-purpose / plain white flour*
- *a few sprigs thyme*
- *a few bay leaves*
- *1 sprig tarragon*
- *3-4 cloves*
- *2 cloves garlic*
- *salt to taste*
- *a few peppercorns*

METHOD

You can use small button mushrooms for this recipe if wild mushrooms are not available. Trim off the ends of the stalks and drop into cold water acidulated with the juice of 1 lemon (if you want to keep cultivated mushrooms especially white, stir a few tablespoons of flour into the water as well, allowing 1 tablespoon flour for each 3 quarts / 5¼ pints / 3 litres water). Heat a large pan full of water with the juice of the remaining lemon and a little salt; when it comes to the boil, drain the mushrooms and add to the boiling water. Remove the mushrooms as soon as the water returns to the boil; drain and leave to cool, covered with a cloth. Prepare the marinade: mix the vinegar with 1 quart / 1¾ pints / 1 litre water and the thyme, bay leaves, tarragon, pepper, cloves and garlic. Bring to the boil and simmer for 10 minutes, then leave to cool.

Pack the mushrooms into jars and pour the marinade over them; if there is not enough to cover them completely, add a little dry white wine. Seal the jars and sterilize for 20 minutes (see page 119).

Good for appetizers and starters or as a relish for boiled or poached meat.

Boletus mushrooms in oil
and marinated chanterelles

Pickled eggplants/aubergines

INGREDIENTS

6½lb / 3kg sound, medium sized dark purple skinned eggplants/aubergines
a sufficient quantity good quality vinegar
1 lemon
a few basil and bay leaves
a few sprigs parsley
a few peppercorns or chilli peppers
salt to taste
olive oil as required

METHOD

Cut the eggplants/aubergines lengthwise into slices about ¼in / ½cm thick; cut away the spongier, seed-bearing flesh from the centre of each eggplant/aubergine as it does not preserve well with this method.

Sprinkle with plenty of salt and pepper. Spread out on a cloth, with or without a weight on top and leave to drain for 4-5 hours. Bring a large pan full of acidulated water (using the lemon juice) to the boil and blanch the slices a few at a time. Spread out on a cloth to dry in full sunlight, turning at least once; when they are dry, pack flat in jars, distributing the basil and parsley leaves, the crumbled bay leaves and a few peppercorns (or crumbled chilli peppers) between the layers.

Fill the jars with good quality vinegar, immersing the contents. Push a wooden or plastic disc into the neck of the jars to keep the vegetables submerged. For the first few days, check and adjust the vinegar level if needed. Trickle a little oil on to the surface of the vinegar.

Choose eggplants/aubergines which are picked (or in the markets) at the height of summer.

Pickled corn on the cob

INGREDIENTS

10-12 baby corn cobs
1 quart / 1¾ pints / 1 litre good quality vinegar
scant ½ cup / 3½oz / 100g sugar
8 peppercorns
3 cloves
1 sprig tarragon
salt to taste

METHOD

Choose corn cobs which are still very pale yellow and about 2½-3in / 6-8 cm long, without any leaves.

Trim and remove any very hard kernels. Add to a pan full of boiling salted water and remove as soon as the water has returned to a fast boil. Drain and leave to dry and cool on clean cloths.

Pack into jars. Boil the vinegar with the sugar, peppercorns, cloves and tarragon for 2 minutes; strain and pour while very hot over the corn, completely covering the cobs. Allow to cool before sealing; keep in a cool, dark place.

Use whenever you would use other pickled vegetables.

Marinated lettuce

INGREDIENTS

4½lb / 2kg escarole (Batavian endive) or Romaine (cos) lettuce

approx ¾ cup / 2oz / 60g finely chopped mixture of parsley, chives, chervil, basil, tarragon

generous 1½ cups / 14fl oz / 400ml dry white wine

scant ½ cup / 3½fl oz / 100ml olive oil

salt to taste

freshly ground pepper to taste

METHOD

Wash the lettuces well and make an intersecting cross incision in the base or bottom of the stalks. Bring plenty of salted water to the boil and plunge the lettuces, whole, into it. Remove as soon as the water has returned to the boil and drain quickly; reserve a little of this blanching liquid.

Heat the wine, oil, herbs, lemon juice, salt and a few peppercorns, adding a little of the reserved blanching liquid; simmer fast for 15 minutes. Remove from the heat and cool.

Transfer the lettuces into jars, cover completely with the marinade, seal and sterilize for 1½ hours (see page 119).

Excellent with roast or broiled/grilled pork, and other types of meat or chicken. Also goes well with scrambled or poached eggs.

Pickled sweet (bell) peppers

INGREDIENTS

6½lb / 3kg plump, sound, ripe sweet peppers

sufficient quantity white wine vinegar

a few basil leaves

a few bay leaves

several sprigs tarragon

salt to taste

METHOD

Quarter the peppers lengthwise, discarding the stalk, seeds and membrane. Wash under cold running water and then blanch for a few seconds in fast boiling salted water; drain and dry in the sun for a few hours.

Pack the peppers in the jars, together with a few basil and bay leaves and, if you have some, a sprig or two of fresh tarragon. Pour in enough vinegar to cover and seal.

Check the vinegar level after a day or two and top up with more so that the peppers are completely immersed.

You can choose a variety of herbs and flavourings: you might like to try small whole (skinned) cloves of garlic, or chop the garlic together with the basil leaves. Eat these peppers on their own or with other pickles, such as mushrooms and artichokes.

Pickled celery

INGREDIENTS

- *4½lb / 2kg (trimmed weight) celery*
- *1 lemon*
- *2 garlic cloves*
- *1 bay leaf*
- *a few cloves*
- *sufficient quantity white wine vinegar*
- *a few basil leaves*
- *a few peppercorns*
- *salt to taste*

METHOD

Remove the outer, greener and tougher stalks and keep for other uses. Wash the tender, paler or white inner part of the celery bunches, snip off the leaves and trim to the correct length to fit into the jars easily (normally about 2½-3in / 6-8cm). Bring a pan of salted water to the boil with the juice of the lemon and a few peppercorns, the garlic cloves, bay leaf and 1 or 2 cloves. Plunge in the celery and blanch for 5 minutes, then drain and spread out to dry for a few hours. Pack neatly into jars and cover with best quality white wine vinegar. Place a few basil leaves and peppercorns in each jar. Seal tightly and keep in cool, dark storage.

These can be a welcome addition to an antipasto or mixed pickled vegetable platter with seafood or cold meat, or they can form part of a Russian salad (cut into very small pieces).

Marinated zucchini/courgettes, Puglia style

INGREDIENTS

- *4½lb / 2kg zucchini/courgettes*
- *a few cloves garlic*
- *2 tablespoons finely chopped parsley*
- *1 sprig basil*
- *1-2 bay leaves*
- *olive oil as required*
- *sufficient quantity white wine vinegar*
- *salt to taste*
- *pepper to taste*

METHOD

Wash the zucchini/courgettes, trim off both ends and cut into ¼in / ½cm rounds. Sprinkle with salt and pepper and leave to lose their excess moisture for 1 hour.

Heat plenty of olive oil; when it is almost smoking hot, fry the zucchini/courgette rounds in batches. As each batch is ready, remove with a slotted spoon, drain and place in a bowl or straight-sided dish in the refrigerator, in layers, spreading each with a mixture of the chopped parsley, garlic and basil and crumbled bay leaves. Pour enough good quality white wine vinegar over them to cover (the last layer should be of zucchini/courgettes). Press down with a small plate and weight; they will keep for several weeks in the refrigerator, provided the vinegar level is topped up. Wrap in plenty of foil to prevent your refrigerator being scented with the garlic.

If you want them to keep longer, pack into jars and sterilize for 20 minutes (see page 119).

Excellent as a starter or with broiled/grilled vegetables.

Dried vegetables and flavoured vinegars

Remind yourself of summer by drying
vegetables or herbs which give
a taste of warmer days
during the long winter months,
or flavour vinegar with your favourite
herbs or fruits for use in delectable
salad dressings all the year round.

Dried mint

Dried Boletus mushrooms

INGREDIENTS

Boletus edulis or other edible type of Boletus (Boletus scaber, Boletus badlus): be careful, some Boletus varieties are poisonous or simply inedible

METHOD

For drying mushrooms (or any vegetables) successfully, you need a very dry, well-ventilated space, under cover (in case of rain and because the vegetables should not dry in direct sunlight). Clean the mushrooms but do not wash or soak them. Cut through them from cap to stalk, making slices about 1/8in / 3-4mm thick; spread out on sheets of untreated paper (not newspaper) in a single layer and cover with a thin, loose-weave cloth or cheesecloth/muslin to protect from insects and dust. Turn the mushrooms frequently so that they dry evenly and completely.

Store in very clean tins lined with greaseproof paper, or in cardboard boxes.

Soak in tepid water before using in risottos, fricassees or casseroles and sautéed, sauced dishes.

Dried eggplants/aubergines

INGREDIENTS

firm, fresh eggplants/aubergines as required

a few bay leaves

salt to taste

a few peppercorns

METHOD

Trim off the remains of the stalk and calyx, wipe with a damp cloth and cut each aubergine lengthwise into slices about ¼in / ½cm thick. Thread the slices on to wooden skewers or thin sticks about 3ft 6in / 1 metre long and then immerse in a large, deep pan full of fast boiling salted water (allow 1oz / 30g salt for every 1 quart / 1¾ pints / 1 litre water), to which a few bay leaves and peppercorns have been added. Blanch in the flavoured water for 2 minutes, then hang up in full sunlight and leave to dry completely. Store in boxes without lids, covered with cloths or cheesecloth/muslin, in a very dry, well-ventilated place.

Soak the eggplants/aubergines in tepid water for 5 minutes before cooking; they can then be fried in oil with garlic and sprinkled with plenty of chopped parsley when they are done.

Dried tomatoes

INGREDIENTS

ripe, but not overripe, very sound tomatoes (the oval, sauce tomatoes, St. Marzano variety, are best for this purpose)

METHOD

Wash the tomatoes and cut in half from top to bottom.

Spread out in a single layer on a working surface or chopping block with the cut sides uppermost. Place in full sunlight and dry; if they seem to be getting too hot, move into the shade for a little while in a well-ventilated spot, or they will lose their juice too quickly through evaporation and their skins will shrink too quickly, letting the flesh brim over and disperse.

When they are completely dry, or dehydrated, store in glass jars with big cork stoppers, or just cover with greaseproof paper fastened with rubber bands.

When using these tomatoes for a sauce or for adding flavour to almost any dish, cook them gently, adding a little water.

Dried tomatoes with basil

INGREDIENTS

generous 6½lb / 3kg small, round, ripe tomatoes, very sound and still firm

bunch freshly picked basil

approx 2 quarts / 3½ pints / 2 litres olive oil

salt to taste

METHOD

Wipe the tomatoes with a damp cloth (do not wash them). Remove their stalks. Cut lengthwise in half, remove the seeds and arrange in a single layer on racks, cut sides uppermost. Sprinkle them with plenty of salt. Place the racks in the sun outdoors and leave all day until sunset. Bring them indoors, and allow the liquid released by each tomato to drain away (give them the gentlest of squeezes if necessary and use paper towels to wipe away the moisture if wished). The next day, place them out in the sun again and bring them in before nightfall, draining off the moisture released each time. After 5 or 6 days of this they should have dried enough (they should have roughly the same softish consistency as dried figs); if not, heat the oven at a low heat for about 15-20 minutes, then place the tomatoes inside and turn it off. Wipe the basil leaves carefully with a damp cloth, spread on paper towels and leave to dry out of doors (in the shade) for a few hours. Match the two halves of each tomato, placing a basil leaf flat between the halves, press firmly together and place the tomatoes in a jar or jars in layers. Completely cover with oil and seal the jars. Top up with more oil the next day if the level has fallen.

Use these tomatoes as an unusual component of a mixed hors d'oeuvre platter or serve with meat (boiled, roasted or grilled) or add to sauces and casseroles.

Dried parsley

INGREDIENTS

a few sprigs parsley

METHOD

Snip off the large stalks of the parsley and discard any damaged leaves. Plunge into a bowl or basin of cold water for a moment or two, swishing around to remove any grit or dirt. Arrange the sprigs in small bunches and tie each with a piece of string. Hang up to dry in full sunshine, bringing them indoors before the dew falls (or cover overnight with waxed paper or polythene to protect from moisture). After 3 or 4 days the parsley should be completely dried. Untie the bunches and snip into small pieces for easy storage in jars or boxes. Keep the parsley in a very dry place.

Very useful during the winter months, on its own or with other herbs. Mint and basil can be dried in the same way.

Herb vinegar

INGREDIENTS

1 quart / 1¾ pints / 1 litre vinegar
2 garlic cloves
a few fresh basil leaves
either small bunch chives or 2 shallots or scallions / spring onions
6-7 peppercorns
2 cloves

METHOD

Chop the herbs and other flavourings very finely and mix with the vinegar. Leave to stand for 24 hours in a china, Pyrex or glass bowl. Strain through a very clean cloth, pour into bottles and seal.

For salad dressings, cold sauces, mayonnaise etc. It can also be used for marinades for red meats, especially game such as venison.

Vinegar flavoured with four herbs

INGREDIENTS

1 quart / 1¾ pints / 1 litre vinegar
2 cloves garlic
1 scallion/spring onion or shallot
pinch thyme
small bunch parsley
sprig fresh rosemary
a few sage leaves
5 peppercorns
1 clove
1 bay leaf

METHOD

Boil all the ingredients together for 5 minutes in a stainless-steel or enamelled saucepan. Pour into bottles when the vinegar is cold and then seal. Instead of boiling all the ingredients together you can pour the boiling vinegar on to all the other ingredients, cover and leave to stand so that the flavours can mingle. Strain and pour into bottles when cold.

Useful for vinaigrette for mixed salads and for hot and cold sauces. You can also use it to pickle vegetables.

It is particularly good when mixed with olive oil and used to dress cold boiled borlotti or pinto beans.

Tarragon vinegar

INGREDIENTS

1 quart / 1¾ pints / 1 litre good quality vinegar
1-2 sprigs tarragon

METHOD

Wash the sprigs of tarragon, shake off excess moisture and place in a bottle of vinegar.

After about 1 week you can use this vinegar for salad dressings or add it to mayonnaise or other cold sauces; particularly good with chicken salads.

Rose petal vinegar

INGREDIENTS

1 quart / 1¾ pints / 1 litre good quality vinegar
3oz / 80g highly scented rose petals

METHOD

Gather the rose petals in the early morning. Rinse them and snip off the yellow tips of the petals where they were joined to the flower centre. Add to a bowl full of vinegar; leave to infuse for 10 days (cover with a cloth). Then strain and pour into bottles. Ready for use immediately.

Good in dressings for potato salads, with cucumbers and zucchini/courgettes etc.

Raspberry-flavoured red wine vinegar

INGREDIENTS

1 quart / 1¾ pints / 1 litre good quality pure red wine vinegar
½-¾lb / 200-300g raspberries
1 lemon

METHOD

Pick the raspberries when they are very ripe; choose clean ones from fairly high canes. Place in a wide-necked bottle, pour in the vinegar and add a couple of pieces of lemon peel (no pith) and a few drops of lemon juice. Cork the bottle, turn upside down slowly once or twice and leave in a cool, dark place to macerate for 2-3 weeks. Afterwards, pour the vinegar into a jelly bag or hair sieve lined with scrupulously clean cheesecloth/muslin and squeeze or push the raspberry flesh through, leaving behind only their seeds. Bottle and seal, storing in cool, dark conditions.

This is a time-honoured recipe which is still prepared in many parts of Italy and France by country people, who make themselves a refreshing drink by mixing a small quantity with fresh water on blazing hot summer days. Also very good when used in a dressing for salads.

Gourmet preserved foods

Certain unusual pickles, preserves and relishes
can be served as a course on their own.
They can also make extremely appetizing
starters or add an original touch
when served with casseroles,
braised meats (particularly veal and beef)
and game dishes.

Sweet-sour onions

Artichokes Italian style

INGREDIENTS

4 artichokes (young and tender)
3 quarts / 5¼ pints / 3 litres water
scant cup / 7fl oz / 200ml fresh lemon juice
1 clove garlic
2 cloves
2 bay leaves
1 small sprig thyme
a few cumin seeds
salt to taste
20 peppercorns

METHOD

Place the water on a moderate heat and bring slowly to the boil with the garlic clove, peppercorns, cloves, bay leaves, lemon juice, thyme, cumin and a generous pinch of salt. While this is heating, trim the artichokes, removing the harder, outer leaves, cutting off some of the stem and scraping what is left; snip off the tips of the leaves with scissors. Work quickly and have the flavoured water boiling fast by the time you are ready to add all the artichokes to it, before they have a chance to discolour. Cook them quickly and remove when they are just tender; add more boiling water if too much evaporates before they are done. Place in a jar or jars and cover with the cooking liquid. Seal and sterilize for 15-20 minutes (see page 119). Keep in a dry, dark place.

You can enjoy these as a starter or as a vegetable with a main course. Good when sautéed with chopped garlic and parsley in oil.

Braised cabbage

INGREDIENTS

4½lb / 2kg green or savoy cabbage
scant ½lb / 200g fresh pork fat in strips or slices
4 carrots
2 onions
2 cloves
1 bouquet garni (thyme and bay leaf)
sufficient quantity bouillon, broth or stock
salt to taste

METHOD

Remove and discard the outer, wilted or damaged leaves of the cabbage; cut the cabbage in quarters, wash and blanch for about 10 minutes in lightly salted boiling water; drain and separate the leaves from the stem or core. Line the bottom of a heavy enamelled iron or earthenware (fireproof) casserole dish with the pork fat strips and add the chopped carrots, the onions (each with a clove stuck in it), and the thyme and bay leaf bouquet. Pour in enough broth or stock to cover these ingredients completely and simmer over a moderate heat for about 2 hours, adding a little more broth when necessary. Pack the cabbage leaves into jars or glazed earthenware pots which can be sealed very tightly together with the broth and all the other ingredients but the onions, cloves and bouquet garni. Stored in the refrigerator, this cabbage will keep for about a week.

Sweet-sour onions

INGREDIENTS

6½lb / 3kg baby (pickling) onions
¼ cup / approx 1oz / 30g seedless white raisins/sultanas
scant cup / 7oz / 200g tomato flesh
1 tablespoon sugar
1 lemon
2 cloves
1 bay leaf
pinch ground cinnamon
pinch freshly ground pepper
generous ½ cup / 5fl oz / 150ml white wine vinegar
generous ½ cup / 5fl oz / 150ml dry white wine
salt to taste

METHOD *(see illustrated instructions on page 196)*

Peel the onions and place in a casserole with the raisins/sultanas, bay leaf, cinnamon, cloves, a teaspoon of grated lemon rind (no pith) and all the juice of the lemon; add the vinegar and white wine, the sugar, the roughly chopped tomato flesh, the pepper and a generous pinch of salt.

Bring to the boil while stirring. Cover the saucepan, and continue cooking on a lower heat or in the oven. When the onions are tender but still whole, taste and add salt or pepper if needed. Transfer them straight into jars, cover with the hot liquid and seal at once. They will keep in the refrigerator for a week. If you want to store them longer, sterilize for 10 minutes (see page 119).

Serve as part of an hors d'oeuvre or with roast or boiled meat.

Piquant onions

INGREDIENTS

6½lb / 3kg peeled baby pickling onions
1¼ cups / 10½oz / 300g sugar
5 cloves
10 peppercorns
2 bay leaves
a few basil leaves
small piece cinnamon bark
1 quart / 1¾ pints / 1 litre white wine vinegar
2 cups / 18fl oz / 500ml white wine
salt to taste

METHOD

Boil the vinegar for about a minute with all the other ingredients except the onions. Bring plenty of salted water to the boil, add the onions and boil for about 3 minutes while stirring. Remove from the heat, cover and leave to stand for 5 minutes, then drain and spread out to dry on a cloth for 3 or 4 hours (cover with another clean cloth) and leave in a fairly cool, well-ventilated place. Pack into jars and cover with the strained vinegar; seal tightly. Sterilize for 10 minutes (see page 119). Instead of sterilizing you can pour the strained vinegar over the onions while still boiling hot, then seal very tightly. Keep cool and away from light.

The onions can be served as cocktail snacks or with appetizers, and the vinegar used for dressings or added to hot sauces.

Green/French beans in tomato sauce

INGREDIENTS

- 4½lb / 2kg young green/French beans
- 2¼lb / 1kg canned or ripe fresh skinned tomatoes
- small pinch sugar
- 1 onion
- 1-2 cloves garlic
- 1 cup / 8fl oz / 225ml olive oil
- salt to taste
- freshly ground pepper to taste

METHOD

Top and tail the beans and rinse in cold water. Heat the oil in a fairly large pan and sauté the chopped onion and the garlic cloves until they just begin to colour, then add the coarsely chopped tomatoes. Simmer for about 2 minutes, then add the beans, a pinch of salt, some pepper and the pinch of sugar (which will counteract the acidity of the tomatoes). Cook gently for 8-10 minutes, stirring and turning frequently. Remove fron the heat and leave to cool before transferring to jars. Seal and sterilize or use the Tyndall method, allowing 25-30 minutes (see pages 119 and 120). Store in a cool, dry and dark place.

These beans should not be kept longer than 6 months. They can be simmered for a few minutes before eating, or the jar can simply be heated in water over a low heat.

Button mushrooms alla cacciatora

INGREDIENTS

- 4½lb / 2kg fresh button mushrooms still tightly closed
- 2 onions
- 2 bay leaves
- 2 sage leaves
- ½lb / 225g ripe tomatoes
- 2-3 cloves garlic
- 2 tablespoons finely chopped parsley
- 1 lemon
- ½ cup / 4fl oz / 125ml white wine
- approx 1 cup / 8fl oz / 225ml olive oil
- salt to taste
- freshly ground pepper to taste

METHOD

Slice off the stalk ends if there is much left or if they are dirty and place the mushrooms in cold water mixed with the juice of the lemon. Pour the olive oil into a large heavy saucepan with the garlic cloves and heat; when the oil is very hot add the drained, dried mushrooms, cooking them fast so that their moisture content evaporates. After 5 minutes, add the finely chopped onions, bay leaves and sage. When almost all the moisture from the mushrooms has evaporated, add the skinned, seeded and coarsely chopped tomatoes, the chopped parsley and the white wine. Discard the garlic cloves. Cook for 3-4 minutes longer, seasoning with salt and pepper. Transfer to jars while still hot, covering the surface with a thin layer of fresh oil. Seal tightly and sterilize for 20 minutes (see page 119). Store under cool, dark conditions. When you want to use them, heat through in a saucepan.

A perfect accompaniment to casseroles, chicken, steaks and veal escalopes.

Green beans
in
tomato sauce
Green beans
in brine

Mushrooms Piedmont style

INGREDIENTS

- *4½lb / 2kg Boletus mushrooms (or cultivated mushrooms)*
- *scant cup / 7fl oz / 200ml olive oil*
- *4 garlic cloves*
- *2 tablespoons finely chopped parsley*
- *1 bay leaf*
- *approx ¼ cup / 1½oz / 30-40g seedless white raisins/sultanas*
- *¼ cup / 2fl oz / 50ml dry white wine*
- *1 small sprig thyme*
- *salt to taste*
- *generous pinch ground pepper*

METHOD

Slice off the earthy end of the stem and trim away the spongy underside of the cap of any large mushrooms. Rinse briefly in cold water, drain and spread out to dry on paper towels for about 30 minutes, then slice fairly thickly.

Crush the garlic cloves almost flat with the side of a knife blade and add to the olive oil, previously heated gently in a large pan. Add the sliced mushrooms, mixing well with a wooden spoon; turn up the heat and add the parsley, bay leaf, thyme, raisins/sultanas and white wine. Stir constantly and reduce the liquid quickly. When it has all evaporated but the mushrooms are still fairly moist, remove from the heat and transfer to jars, discarding the garlic. Press down gently, cover the surface with a thin film of fresh oil and seal tightly.

Sterilize the jars for 45 minutes or use the Tyndall method (see pages 119 and 120).

A very elegant and unusual starter, particularly when the Boletus wild mushrooms are used.

Mixed sweet-sour vegetable medley

INGREDIENTS

- *1lb / 500g young carrots*
- *½-¾lb / 300g tender celery*
- *½-¾lb / 300g eggplants/aubergines*
- *¾lb / 400g zucchini/courgettes*
- *1½ cups / ¾lb / 350g sugar*
- *2 cups / 18fl oz / 500ml wine vinegar or good malt vinegar*
- *a few leaves fresh basil*
- *2 bay leaves*
- *a few peppercorns*
- *salt to taste*

METHOD

Peel the carrots, remove the strings from the celery, and slice off both ends of the eggplants/aubergines and the zucchini/courgettes. Cut everything into small dice and blanch each batch of vegetables for a few minutes in boiling salted water. They must still be crisp when drained; none of them is likely to take more than 5 minutes' blanching. Drain and mix them together in a large stainless-steel preserving pan.

Add the sugar, vinegar, bay leaves and a few very coarsely crushed peppercorns. Bring to the boil while stirring. Simmer, skimming when necessary, until the vinegar has evaporated and the vegetables form a dense mixture but not a mush. Stir in the basil leaves, remove from the heat and ladle the vegetables straight into warmed jars. Seal tightly, cool slowly (wrapped in cloths if wished) and store in a cool, dry, dark place.

These can be eaten without any further embellishment or mixed with other cooked vegetables: potatoes, onions, green/French beans.

Green/French beans in brine and in tomato sauce

Eggplants/aubergines with herbs and tomatoes

INGREDIENTS

- 2¼lb / 1kg sound, firm eggplants/aubergines
- 1 tablespoon pickled capers
- 4-5 garlic cloves
- 2¼lb / 1kg ripe tomatoes
- 1 tablespoon finely chopped parsley
- generous pinch oregano
- a few leaves fresh basil
- approx 1½ quarts / 2 pints 13fl oz / 1½ litres vinegar
- olive oil as required
- freshly ground pepper to taste
- salt to taste

METHOD

Trim off the tops of the eggplants/aubergines, then wash and dry. Dice and place in a colander with a plate and weight on top, having first sprinkled them liberally with salt and pepper, and leave to release their bitter liquid.

Bring a large pan of the vinegar mixed with an equal volume of water to the boil and blanch the drained eggplants/aubergines for a few seconds only; drain well. Heat plenty of olive oil with the garlic cloves, chopped capers, peeled and seeded tomatoes, parsley, oregano and basil leaves. Once the garlic has coloured slightly, add the eggplants/aubergines and sauté briskly for 3-4 minutes, stirring and turning. Remove from the heat and put straight into jars, pouring a thin layer of fresh olive oil on top. Seal tightly and sterilize for 20-25 minutes (see page 119). Keep in a cool, dark place.

Before you eat the eggplants/aubergines, sauté them briefly, adding a pinch of sugar to counteract the slightly bitter taste.

Sautéed eggplants/aubergines

INGREDIENTS

- 2¼lb / 1kg sound, firm eggplants/aubergines
- 2-3 garlic cloves
- 2 tablespoons finely chopped parsley
- a few leaves fresh basil
- pinch oregano
- approx 1½ quarts / 2 pints 13fl oz / 1½ litres good quality vinegar
- approx 1 cup / 8fl oz / 225ml olive oil
- salt to taste
- freshly ground pepper to taste

METHOD

Trim and wash the eggplants/aubergines; cut in half, scooping out the spongier flesh in the centre. Cut into fairly large dice but do not skin. Sprinkle with salt and pepper and place in a colander covered with a plate and weight to degorge. Bring the vinegar to the boil in a stainless-steel pan and blanch the eggplants/aubergines in several batches, for about 1 minute each. Heat the oil in a large skillet/frying pan with the garlic cloves and, when the garlic starts to colour, add the eggplants/aubergines and sauté for about 2 minutes before stirring in the parsley, basil and oregano. Remove from the heat, spoon into jars and cover the surface with a thin film of fresh olive oil. Seal tightly and sterilize for 10-15 minutes (see page 119). Keep in a dry, dark place.

A vegetable ready to serve with roast meat and poultry.

Green olive and anchovy compote

INGREDIENTS

- *generous 6½lb / 3kg fresh green olives*
- *about 6 anchovy fillets*
- *a few basil leaves*
- *generous pinch oregano*
- *small piece hot red (chilli) pepper*
- *approx 2 tablespoons capers*
- *1 lemon*
- *approx 2 quarts / 3½ pints / 2 litres olive oil*
- *salt to taste*

METHOD

Pit/stone the olives (use a patent olive pitter/stoner) and place in a deep china or plastic bowl; cover with cold water, which should come at least 4in / 10cm above the olives. Leave to soak for 5-6 days, changing the water each day. When this process of sweetening the olives is completed, drain the olives and tip on to a clean cloth; cover with another cloth and press down gently to absorb all excess moisture. Place between two fresh dry cloths and leave to dry in a well-ventilated place for 4-5 hours.

Arrange the olives in layers in jars, alternating them with pieces of anchovy fillet, the basil leaves, oregano, pieces of chilli pepper, capers and a few drops of lemon juice, a pinch of salt and some oil. Press each layer down gently before covering with the next. When each jar is almost full, press down firmly and then top up with oil to cover completely. Cover with a waxed paper disc, then with a wooden or plastic disc to keep the olives below the oil. Store in a dry, dark place.

For decorating canapés and garnishing salads and hard-boiled eggs.

Black olive spread

INGREDIENTS

- *¾lb / 350g pitted/stoned black olives*
- *5oz / 150g salted anchovy fillets*
- *scant ¼lb / 100g pickled capers*
- *scant cup / 7fl oz / 200ml olive oil*
- *1 lemon*
- *1 tablespoon brandy*
- *generous pinch freshly ground pepper*
- *salt to taste*

METHOD

For the best consistency you should pound the olives in a stone mortar (difficult to find these days). Otherwise place the olives, anchovies (use drained canned anchovies if salted ones are not available) and capers in a food processor and process until they have turned to a very fine paste. It should be very smooth, but sieve if necessary.

Place the purée in a bowl and gradually beat in the olive oil, adding it in a very thin trickle as if you were making a mayonnaise; towards the end of the oil add a very little at a time, to give the olive paste a chance to absorb it. Add the lemon juice, brandy and pepper and salt if necessary. Pack tightly into small jars and cover the surface of each with a disc of waxed or sulphur-treated paper. Seal the jars and keep in a cool, dark place.

An extremely useful standby for making canapés, spreading on toast, or stuffing hardboiled eggs or small tomatoes.

Olives in tuna, tomato and herb sauce

INGREDIENTS

- *2¼lb / 1kg olives, pickled in brine*
- *¼lb / 100g salted/anchovy fillets*
- *½ cup / 3½oz / 100g canned tuna*
- *1 tablespoon finely chopped parsley*
- *1 tablespoon finely crumbled dried hot red (chilli) peppers*
- *scant ¼lb / 100g chopped pickled capers (in brine or vinegar)*
- *1¼ cups / 10oz / 300g skinned, seeded, chopped tomatoes*
- *1 cup / 9fl oz / 250ml olive oil*
- *a few fresh basil leaves*
- *4-5 cloves garlic*

METHOD

Pit/stone the olives using the appropriate gadget; slice into rounds. Chop all the other ingredients and mix together. Arrange layers of olives, covered by layers of the chopped mixture, in jars, sprinkling each with a little oil. When the jars are full, top up with oil, seal tightly and sterilize for 30 minutes (see page 119). Keep in a cool, dark place.

A mixture which can be used with other hors d'oeuvres, or as a stuffing for certain vegetables and, sparingly, as a dressing on freshly cooked, steaming hot pasta.

Puglia sweet (bell) peppers

INGREDIENTS

- *10 fleshy sweet (bell) peppers*
- *10oz / 300g canned anchovy fillets*
- *scant ½lb / 200g salted capers*
- *4-5 cloves garlic*
- *small bunch parsley*
- *small bunch fresh basil*
- *small quantity olive oil*
- *approx 1 quart / 1¾ pints / 1 litre white wine vinegar*
- *salt to taste*

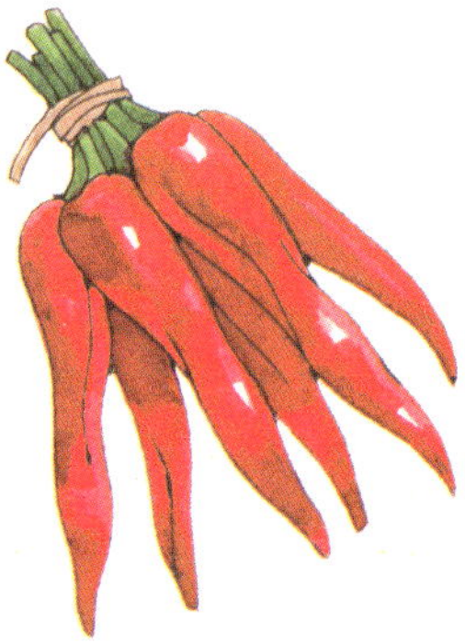

METHOD *(see illustrated instructions on page 197)*

Wash the peppers thoroughly, dry, cut in half lengthwise and discard the stalk, seeds and membrane before slicing into fairly broad strips.

Bring the vinegar to the boil (you may need more than the listed quantity) with a generous pinch of salt. Sprinkle the peppers gradually into the fast boiling vinegar to prevent the liquid from cooling. Boil for about 10 minutes, remove with a slotted spoon and spread out on clean cloths.

Place a layer of pepper strips in the bottom of a jar, sprinkle with a few slivers of garlic, a few capers and pieces of anchovy fillet and several basil and parsley leaves (washed and dried first). Continue layering the ingredients to within about ¾in / 2cm of the top of the jar. Pour in sufficient oil to completely cover the peppers. Seal the jar and leave for at least 24 hours before checking the oil level (which will sink as it permeates the layers of peppers). Top up with more oil so that the peppers remain completely immersed. Seal tightly and store in a cool, dark place.

Wait at least 1 month before tasting.

Whenever you are preserving vegetables in oil, do not be tempted to buy cheap olive oil; buy only the best. It will not be wasted as you can use it for salad dressings and the vegetables will taste superb.

Stuffed red and yellow peppers

INGREDIENTS

- *generous 6½lb / 3kg sound, plump red and yellow sweet (bell) peppers*
- *2 quarts / 3½ pints / 2 litres good quality wine vinegar*
- *20-30 anchovy fillets*
- *a few leaves fresh basil*
- *4-5 cloves garlic*
- *approx 2 quarts / 3½ pints / 2 litres olive oil*
- *salt to taste*

METHOD

Heat the peppers over the gas burner, speared on a carving fork, and turn (or place under the broiler/grill) to scorch the outer skin, which will then be easy to peel off. Cut off the stem and surround, remove the seeds and membrane and spread out to dry for 1 hour. Blanch very briefly in the boiling vinegar (1 minute should be enough or they will be mushy).

Drain and slice lengthwise into quarters or sixths; place an anchovy fillet on the inner side of each portion and then roll up and pack tightly into jars. Place a basil leaf and a sliver of garlic on top of each layer and cover completely with oil. Seal tightly; check the oil level after a few days and top up if necessary. Put away in a cool, dark place.

A splendidly unusual snack or addition to a mixed plate of savouries.

Peperonata

INGREDIENTS

- *2¼lb / 1kg sound, fleshy sweet (bell) peppers*
- *1lb / 500g tomatoes*
- *1 clove garlic*
- *2 onions*
- *1 bay leaf*
- *pinch sugar*
- *½ cup / 4fl oz / 125ml olive oil*
- *salt to taste*
- *pepper to taste*

METHOD

Remove the thin, outer skins of the peppers as described in the preceding recipe, then cut the pepper lengthwise into strips about ½in / 1cm thick. Sauté the chopped garlic and onion in a little olive oil until the onion is pale golden brown; add the peppers, the peeled, seeded tomatoes, salt and freshly ground pepper to taste, a pinch of sugar and the bay leaf. Simmer gently for 5 minutes and then leave to cool. Pour the sweet pepper mixture into jars and add a few basil leaves. Seal tightly and sterilize for 2 hours (see page 119), or use the Tyndall method (see page 120).

Heat the peperonata to boiling before serving with boiled, poached or roasted meats, poultry or ham. Equally delicious when cold.

Puglia sweet (bell) peppers

Gourmet's peas

INGREDIENTS
4½lb / 2kg hulled/shelled peas
2 onions
generous 1lb / 500g any variety lettuce or salad greens
small quantity olive oil
to taste salt
generous pinch freshly ground pepper

METHOD

Sauté the chopped onion in a little oil and when it has softened and started to colour, add the trimmed, washed and dried lettuce, cut into strips. Sauté for a minute or two. Add the rinsed and drained peas and season with salt and pepper. Add a little hot water if necessary and boil for 10 minutes. When the peas are almost done, remove from the heat and pour into jars (there should be just enough liquid to keep the peas moist). Seal tightly and sterilize for 1 hour (see page 119).

The peas can be warmed just as they are or, for a special touch, sauté diced streaky bacon or pancetta in a little oil or butter until just crisp and add to the heated peas.

Tomato paste/purée with vegetables

INGREDIENTS
11lb / 5kg tomatoes
2 onions
2 sticks/stalks celery
2 carrots
a few bay leaves
3 garlic cloves
1 small sprig thyme
a few leaves fresh basil
1 teaspoon sugar for each 2¼lb / 1kg of tomatoes
½ cup / 4fl oz / 125ml olive oil
salt to taste
pinch freshly ground pepper

METHOD

Cut the tomatoes in half, squeeze out excess juice and seeds and leave to drain for 30 minutes.

Sauté the chopped onion, celery and carrots in oil in a large deep pan; add the herbs, the slightly crushed garlic cloves and the tomatoes, and simmer until the sauce has thickened considerably (the more you reduce it, the better it will be). Stir in the sugar, salt and pepper. Discard the garlic cloves and herbs and push the tomato mixture through a fine sieve. Pour the smooth, thick paste or purée into jars and sterilize for about 30 minutes (see page 119).

If you add salicylic acid to the purée there is no need to sterilize. Allow a generous pinch or 1g for each 2¼lb / 1kg of tomato paste/purée.

Curried leeks

INGREDIENTS

- *4½lb / 2kg leeks*
- *1 tablespoon mild curry powder*
- *2 tablespoons seedless white raisins/sultanas*
- *2-3 bay leaves*
- *2 dessert apples (such as Russet)*
- *small quantity dry white wine*
- *½ cup / 4fl oz / 125ml olive oil*
- *salt to taste*
- *generous pinch freshly ground pepper*

METHOD

Trim and wash the leeks very thoroughly, cutting them into 1½in / 4cm sections (cut the leeks in half lengthwise if they are very large). Arrange the leeks in a single layer in a large shallow fireproof dish. Sprinkle with salt, pepper and the curry powder mixed with the oil, the crumbled bay leaf, raisins/sultanas, and the peeled, sliced apples; pour in enough white wine to come half way up the leeks. Cover completely with a sheet of greaseproof paper, weighting this down with the lid, and heat until the wine boils; then place in a pre-heated hot oven for 15 minutes.

Drain all the moisture from the leeks and pack into jars. Push the cooking juices and wine and all the other ingredients through a sieve into a small saucepan; boil for 2 minutes while stirring; the resulting sauce should be moderately thick. Pour it straight on to the leeks: it should cover them but the contents should remain below the top of the jar. Seal tightly and sterilize for 20 minutes (see page 119). Put away in a cool, dark place.

A really exquisite starter or vegetable dish.

Pickled vegetable brochettes

INGREDIENTS

- *4½lb / 2kg small eggplants/aubergines*
- *4½lb / 2kg firm, fleshy red and yellow sweet (bell) peppers*
- *3¼lb / 1½kg baby onions*
- *4½lb / 2kg medium-sized zucchini/courgettes*
- *a few leaves fresh basil*
- *2-3 bay leaves*
- *4-5 cloves garlic*
- *sufficient quantity white wine vinegar*
- *a few peppercorns*
- *6-7 cloves*
- *small piece cinnamon bark*
- *salt to taste*

METHOD

Wash the vegetables carefully and dry. Bring a large pan of salted water to the boil with a few peppercorns (coarsely crushed), the cloves and cinnamon. Slice the eggplants/aubergines and zucchini/courgettes into rounds ¼in / ½cm thick; cut the peppers into squares about the same size as the eggplant/aubergine and zucchini/courgette rounds; peel the onion. Blanch the zucchini/courgettes in the fast boiling water for about 5 minutes and drain: they should still be crisp. Spread out on a cloth to dry and cool. When the water has returned to the boil, blanch the peppers for 3 minutes, drain and cool. Repeat with the onions, then with the eggplants/aubergines.

Thread the vegetables on to wooden skewers (about 2in / 5cm long), alternating types of vegetables and including the basil leaves among them. Place the assembled skewers in large jars. Boil the vinegar for a minute or less after adding the crushed cloves of garlic, a few coarsely crushed peppercorns and the bay leaves; pour through a conical sieve, straight into the jars, to cover the vegetables completely. Leave to cool before sealing and keep in a cool, dark place.

Ideal as a starter or an accompaniment for barbecued meat.

Truffles in wine

INGREDIENTS

whatever you can afford in the way of truffles
dry white wine as required
dry Marsala (fortified wine) as required

METHOD

Rub the truffles with a coarse, rough cloth or scrub with a soft clean brush; do not rinse or wash at all (remember wine has antiseptic properties). Bring the wine and Marsala, in equal parts, just to boiling point. Pack the truffles into jars, and as soon as the wine mixture boils pour it straight over them, making sure they are completely covered. Seal tightly and sterilize for 30 minutes (see page 119). It is best to use small jars since, quite apart from the expense, you will probably only need to use these truffles in small quantities and they must be consumed very soon after the jars have been opened.

Not only can you use the truffles to impart a delectable flavour and aroma to a wide range of dishes, but the wine will have taken up the scent of the truffles too, so use it for sauces.

Scorzonera/salsify, Piedmont style

INGREDIENTS

4½lb / 2kg peeled scorzonera/black salsify
generous ½ cup / 5fl oz / 150ml olive oil
1 lemon
3 bay leaves
1 small sprig thyme
6-8 peppercorns
1 small piece cinnamon bark
generous cup / 9fl oz / 250ml dry white wine
salt to taste

METHOD

As you peel the sticks of scorzonera/salsify, immerse these in a large bowl of cold water acidulated with the juice of the lemon; cut the roots into sections about 2in / 5cm long, as even in thickness as possible (some you will have to cut lengthwise in half). Bring 2 quarts / 3½ pints / 2 litres of the acidulated water to the boil in a large pan together with all the other ingredients and a few pieces of the lemon peel. Add the scorzonera/salsify and boil gently for about 15 minutes, removing any scum and stirring from time to time. Remove from the heat and transfer the liquid and scorzonera/salsify into a bowl to cool; when cold arrange in jars, packing as tightly as possible. Strain the cooking liquid and pour over the scorzonera/salsify to cover. If there is not enough, have a little boiled, cooled, salted water ready to top up.

Seal tightly and sterilize for 45 minutes or use the Tyndall method (see pages 119 and 120).

Drain the preserving liquid and eat, hot or cold, with a dressing of olive oil, lemon juice and plenty of freshly ground pepper.

Peperonata

Spinach Piedmont style

INGREDIENTS

4½lb / 2kg spinach
scant ¼ cup / 1oz / 25g seedless white raisins/sultanas
1 cup / 8fl oz / 225ml white wine
freshly ground pepper to taste
salt to taste

METHOD

Wash the spinach thoroughly in several changes of fresh cold water. Soak the raisins/sultanas in the white wine for 2 hours to soften. Drain the spinach well and place in a stainless-steel or enamelled pan with the raisins/sultanas, the wine and a pinch of salt and pepper, and bring rapidly to the boil. As soon as all the leaves have wilted, remove from the heat and transfer to the jars with a little of the cooking liquid. Do not seal the jars until after the spinach has cooled completely.

Seal tightly and sterilize for 15 minutes (see page 119). Allow the jars to cool slowly in the sterilizer, then store in a cool, dark place.

Heat very gently before serving with a variety of meat and poultry dishes, eggs and cheese sauce, etc.

Vegetable Caprice

INGREDIENTS

2¼lb / 1kg eggplants/aubergines
3¼lb / 1½kg yellow, red and green sweet (bell) peppers
2¼lb / 1kg any type of edible wild or cultivated mushrooms
2¼lb / 1kg carrots
2¼lb / 1kg white celery
a few sprigs tarragon
sufficient quantity white wine vinegar
small quantity olive oil
2-3 cloves
a few small pieces cinnamon bark
a few peppercorns
salt to taste

METHOD

Trim, wash and dry the vegetables. Keep them separate from each other, cutting them into fairly large julienne strips (about 1½in / 4cm long). Do not use the central, seed-bearing, spongy part of the eggplants/aubergines. Bring plenty of vinegar to the boil with a little salt, coarsely ground pepper, cloves and the pieces of cinnamon. Start by blanching the celery for 1 minute, remove with a slotted spoon, then drain on a cloth. Blanch the mushrooms, carrots, peppers and eggplants/aubergines in the same way, separately. All the vegetables should still be crisp when blanched, and times will vary from 1 to 3 minutes. When they have all drained, pack into jars (having first mixed them well) with the tarragon leaves. Press down well and add a few crushed peppercorns. Stop when the jars are full to within about 1in / 2½cm from the top and cover with oil, topping up with more when you have waited for it to sink into the vegetables. Seal well and store in a dry, dark place.

Make interesting cold sauces with these vegetables: citronette, mayonnaise, sauce aurore, rémoulade etc.

Sweet-sour mixed vegetable relish

INGREDIENTS

- 2¼lb / 1kg eggplants/aubergines
- 1lb / 500g zucchini/courgettes
- 1lb / 500g onions
- 1lb / 500g tender white celery
- 2¼lb / 1kg ripe sweet peppers
- 2 cups / 1lb / 500g sugar
- 1 quart / 1¾ pints / 1 litre white wine vinegar
- pinch ground cinnamon
- ¼ cup / 2fl oz / 50ml grappa or marc
- 5-6 cloves
- freshly ground pepper to taste
- 1 tablespoon / scant 1 oz / 20g salt

METHOD

Rinse and trim all the vegetables. Peel and dice the eggplants/aubergines, sprinkle with salt and pepper and place in a colander covered with a plate and weight for 2 hours to release the bitter juice. Dice the zucchini/courgettes, add to boiling, salted water and cook for 5 minutes, then drain. Chop the celery into fairly small pieces, boil in lightly salted water for 10 minutes and drain; do likewise with the sweet (bell) peppers, first removing and discarding the seeds and pith. Place all these vegetables in the preserving pan; add the finely chopped onions, vinegar, cinnamon, cloves and freshly ground pepper. Bring to the boil while stirring continuously. Remove any scum and continue cooking until the vegetables are very tender and the liquid has almost entirely evaporated.

Remove from the heat; sieve or put through a vegetable mill and return the purée to the preserving pan. Add the sugar and grappa or marc and cook over a low heat while stirring until very thick (a jam consistency). Remove from the heat and ladle into jars.

Especially good with broiled/grilled meat, roasted game and spit-roasted chicken.

Marinated zucchini/courgettes, Rumanian style

INGREDIENTS

- 6½lb / 3kg firm, sound zucchini/courgettes
- scant 1½ cups / 12fl oz / 350ml olive oil
- 6 lemons
- 5 scallions/spring onions
- 1 teaspoon peppercorns
- generous pinch thyme
- 2 bay leaves
- pinch basil
- 1 clove garlic
- salt to taste

METHOD

Cut both ends from the zucchini/courgettes but do not peel, just wipe with a damp cloth; slice into approx ⅜in / 1cm thick rounds. Make a marinade by placing all the other ingredients together with the coarsely chopped onions in the preserving pan containing 1½ quarts / 2½ pints / 1½ litres water. As soon as this marinade comes to a fast boil, blanch the zucchini/courgettes for a few seconds in batches, keeping the marinade boiling hard all the time; allow it to boil fast again before adding the next batch. As you remove the blanched vegetables, spread them out on clean, dry cloths, preferably not overlapping.

Place the dry zucchini/courgettes in jars in even layers; do not press down tightly. Allow the marinade to continue boiling while doing this; then remove from the heat, strain and pour into the jars to come no lower than ⅜in / 1cm below the lip of each jar. Seal and sterilize for 15 minutes (see page 119).

Serve as a starter or with boiled meat or poached fish.

How it's done – step by step

For the absolute beginner,
and also for the expert who has an occasional problem,
here are some key recipes,
illustrated with step-by-step photographs
to ensure correct results.

ORANGE AND LEMON MARMALADE

1

2

3

4

5

1 *Pare off the peel and then remove and discard the bitter pith surrounding the oranges and lemons.*

2 *Place the orange and lemon flesh and their shredded peels in the preserving pan; add the sugar.*

3 *Bring to the boil and cook, stirring continuously with a wooden spoon.*

4 *Remove the scum while cooking the marmalade, using a fine mesh skimmer or perforated ladle.*

5 *Ladle the hot marmalade into the prepared jars, seal tightly and store in a cool place.*

CITRON MARMALADE

1

2

3

4

5

1 *Cut the citrons in half lengthwise and soak in cold water for 2 days.*

2 *Simmer the citrons in water until their rinds are soft, then drain well.*

3 *Allow to cool on a wooden chopping block or work surface before cutting into fairly large pieces.*

4 *Make the sugar syrup with water and sugar, add the citrons and simmer gently.*

5 *Add rum to the jam when done, ladle into jars and seal tightly.*

GREEN TOMATO JAM

1

2

3

4

5

1 *Cut the tomatoes in half, squeeze out the seeds and excess water, then cut into pieces.*

2 *Add the sugar and the juice of two lemons and peel of one, and stir well.*

3 *Transfer to the preserving pan and when the mixture has thickened, remove from heat.*

4 *Place a spoonful of jam on a cold plate and tilt; if the jam slides down the plate slowly, it is ready.*

5 *Ladle or pour the hot jam into prepared jars and seal at once.*

ORANGES PRESERVED IN ALCOHOL

1

2

3

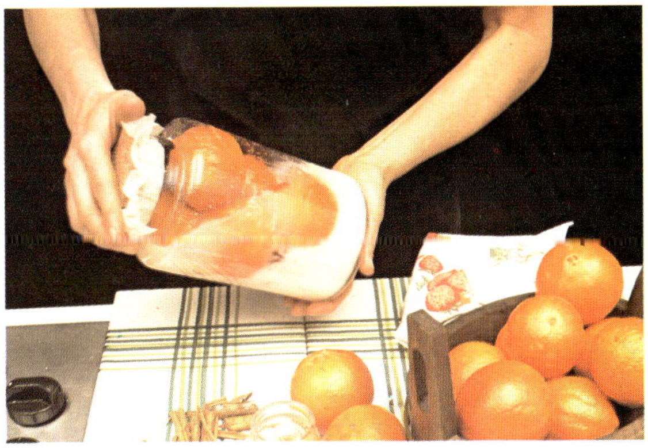

4

5

1 *Pierce the oranges deeply in four or five widely spaced places with a large needle or fork.*

2 *Place in jars, cover with superfine/caster sugar and add the lemon peel and other flavourings.*

3 *Pour the 95° spirit on to the oranges and seal the jar tightly.*

4 *Shake the jar gently from side to side, holding it as shown.*

5 *After 6 months the oranges are ready to serve as a dessert; the liquid can be bottled.*

GRAPES IN GRAPPA

1

2

3

4

5

1 *Snip the individual grapes off the bunch, leaving a fraction of an inch (about 1 mm) of stalk attached.*

2 *Rinse briefly in cold water, drain and dry gently but thoroughly in a very clean cloth.*

3 *Place the grapes in the jars with strips of lemon peel and pieces of cinnamon; then add the sugar.*

4 *Pour in sufficient grappa (marc made from grape skins and stalks) to cover all the grapes.*

5 *After about a month you can serve the grapes as the perfect finish to a dinner party menu.*

HOW IT'S DONE — STEP BY STEP

DRIED APPLES

1

2

3

4

5

1 *Peel the apples. Russet, Reinette, Golden Delicious or Morgan dry best; they must be very sound and ripe.*

2 *Core carefully, using an apple corer; keep them as neat as possible.*

3 *Slice into rings just over ½in / 1cm thick. Work quickly and ensure even thickness.*

4 *Spread out on cookie sheets or metal trays and place in the oven, preheated to 104°F / 40°C.*

5 *Remove when partially dried. Leave to dry further. Then store in open wooden boxes lined with paper.*

ARTICHOKES IN LIGHT BRINE

1

2

3

4

5

6

7

8

9

10

1 *Strip off the outer leaves and cut off the pointed tips. Place in acidulated water.*

2 *Pack the prepared artichokes into jars, leaving as few gaps as possible.*

3 *Pour the boiling water over the artichokes to cover; seal tightly before sterilizing.*

4 *Place the slotted disc in the bottom of the sterilizer, on which the jars will be placed.*

5 *If the jars are small, try to accommodate two layers (place another disc between the layers).*

6 *Slot the cover in place and rotate until engaged and hermetically sealed.*

7 *Set the pressure gauge to a temperature of 248°F / 120°C before placing on the hob or burner.*

8 *Turn on the heat, bring to the boil or up to pressure and cook for 10 minutes.*

9 *Turn off the heat, waiting for the pressure to fall to zero before removing the lid.*

10 *Allow the jars to cool completely in the water before removing.*

CAULIFLOWER IN OIL

1

2

3

4

5

1 *Cut off the florets from the cauliflower; they should be quite small and about the same size.*

2 *Boil the vinegar with the wine, peppercorns, cinnamon bark, lemon peel and bay leaves.*

3 *Add the cauliflower florets to the fast boiling vinegar and simmer gently for about 5 minutes.*

4 *Drain the cauliflower well, dry and then pack firmly into preserving jars.*

5 *Pour in enough best quality, first pressing olive oil to completely cover the cauliflower.*

BUTTON MUSHROOMS IN VINEGAR

1

2

3

4

5

1 *Add the trimmed mushrooms to a large pan of boiling, salted and acidulated water.*

2 *Pour sufficient vinegar into a fairly large pan, adding the cinnamon, cloves and bay leaves.*

3 *Drain the water from the mushrooms, pat dry in a clean cloth and then place in jars.*

4 *Boil the vinegar for a few minutes and pour through a sieve, covering the mushrooms completely.*

5 *Add a few peppercorns and a pinch of tarragon, and cover the surface with a thin film of olive oil.*

SWEET-SOUR ONIONS

1

2

3

4

5

1 *Place the prepared onions in a heatproof dish; add the spices and herbs and sprinkle with lemon juice.*

2 *Pour in the vinegar and the white wine and sprinkle with sugar, stirring well.*

3 *Add the shredded or chopped fresh, de-seeded tomatoes (or use canned tomatoes).*

4 *Bring to the boil while stirring with a wooden spoon.*

5 *Transfer the onion mixture into very clean dry jars while still hot and ladle in plenty of liquid.*

PUGLIA SWEET (BELL) PEPPERS

1

2

3

4

5

1 *Bring plenty of vinegar to the boil and add the peppers, cut into strips, in several instalments.*

2 *Simmer for about 10 minutes, lift out with a slotted spoon and spread out to dry on a clean cloth.*

3 *Arrange a layer of peppers, sprinkle with garlic slivers, capers, anchovy fillets...*

4 *...and some basil and parsley. Continue layering, pressing down gently as you go.*

5 *When the jars are full, add enough olive oil to cover the peppers completely.*

BOTANICAL GUIDE

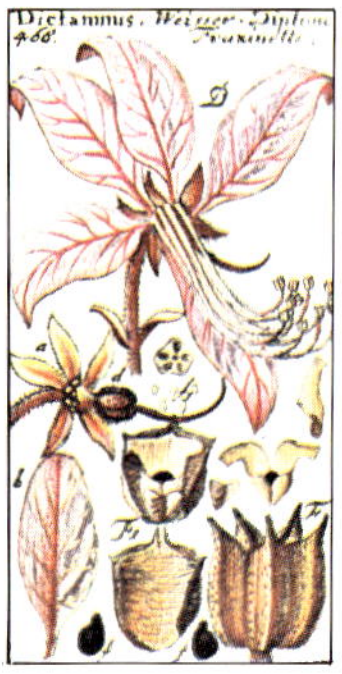
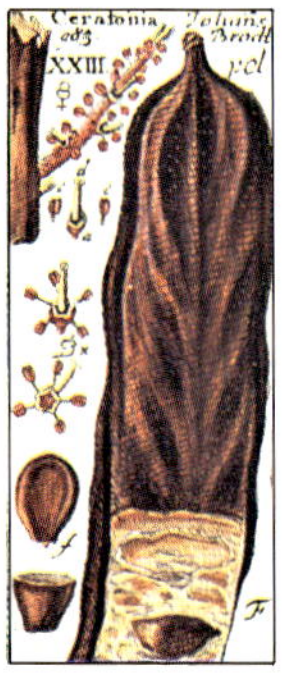

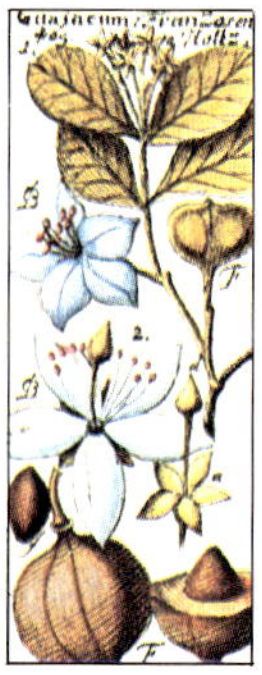
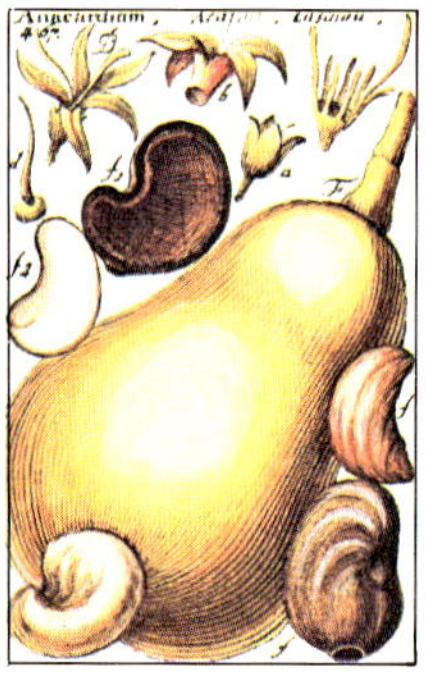

We have kept the last few pages for the real stars of the show, the plants which produce the raw material for the preserves covered in this book. The fruits we have chosen for these brief descriptions are apricot, orange, cherry, strawberry, apple, peach, currant (black, red and white) and grape. The vegetables are artichoke, carrot, aubergine, bell (sweet) pepper, tomato (strictly speaking a fruit) and pumpkin. The profiles cover the families to which each plant belongs, the region where it originated, a detailed description of its leaves, flowers and fruits, when these appear and how to use them, and a guide to some of the best varieties for preserving.

APRICOT (*Prunus armeniaca*)

Family
Rosaceae
Origin
Northern China
Description
Standard tree grows about 20ft (6-7m) tall with an elegant spherical crown
Leaves
Long leafstalks bear leaves which can be ovate or heart-shaped, smooth, bright green
Flowers
Large pink blossoms usually growing singly; white or palest pink appearing before the leaves
Flowering
Very early spring
Fruit
Round, yellow or orange-yellow drupe with a velvety skin; the flesh is a yellow and succulent pulp; ripening in summer
Cultivation
Mainly for the fruit
Varieties
USA: *Early Golden, Moorpark*. Warmer zones: *Blenheim (Royal), Tilton, Wenatchee.*
Cooler zones: *Moongold*. UK: *Moorpark*

ORANGE *(Citrus)*

Family
Rutaceae
Origin
Asia
Description
Tree which varies in height: standard 20-25ft (6-7.6m); dwarf 8-10ft (2.4-3m)
Leaves
Large, leathery, dark and evergreen. Ovate with smooth or sawtoothed edges
Flowers
White with a heady scent (bitter or Seville oranges have an even more fragrant perfume)
Flowering
Late spring, early summer
Fruit
Round or oval, very bright deep yellow or orange when ripe; juicy yellow flesh (tinged with red in blood oranges), divided into segments
Cultivation
As a fruit tree and ornamental tree. Flowers and leaves of bitter orange also used for essential oils and orange flower water or distilled essence
Varieties
USA (and UK imported): *Torocco, Ruby* (canning, bottling). UK: *Seville* (bitter) oranges for marmalade

SWEET CHERRY *(Prunus avium)*

Family
Rosaceae
Origin
Temperate regions of northern hemisphere
Description
Trees can attain height of 65ft (20m); tall, straight trunk with very dark bark
Leaves
Ovate or reverse ovate, varying in length, saw-toothed, often drooping; dark green
Flowers
Umbels of 2-6 flowers on long stalks, white or pink petals, reddish calyx; delicate fragrance
Flowering
Early spring
Fruit
Round or egg-shaped, shiny skin; yellow, yellow and red, red or purplish depending on variety. Sweet or slightly sour. Ripening in June or July, depending on region and variety
Cultivation
As a fruit tree
Varieties
USA & UK: *Bing, Black Tartarian, Lambert, Windsor, Royal Ann (Napoleon), Schmidt's Bigarreau.* (Mainly for jams and sweet canned or bottled cherries)

ALPINE STRAWBERRY *(Fragaria vesca)*

Family
Rosaceae
Origin
Warm and temperate regions of northern hemisphere, central America and certain areas of Andes and isolated regions in southern hemisphere
Description
Perennial, erect, herbaceous plant; rhizomes with runners
Leaves
Thin, light green, composed of three leaflets, ovate with large, sharp serrations
Flowers
Borne on pedicel, five small white petals
Flowering
Season varies, according to variety
Fruit
Spherical or ovoid berry consisting of fleshy receptacle, usually red, juicy pulp bearing numerous tiny hard seeds (ovaries) embedded in surface
Cultivation
For the fruit
Varieties
Many hybrids and varieties of *Fragaria vesca* are cultivated. USA: *Catskill.* Warmer regions: *Pocahontas, Tennessee Beauty, Florida 90, Missionary.* UK: *Cambridge Rival* (particularly good for jam)

APPLE *(Pirus malus)*

Family
Rosaceae
Origin
Europe, Asia, North America
Description
Tree or shrub with spreading, rounded crown
Leaves
Deciduous, ovate, sometimes palmate or lobed with sawtoothed edges; usually bright green
Flowers
Solitary or in clusters, white or white tinged with pink, red or reddish crimson, single or double
Flowering
Usually April or May
Fruit
Round or oval, varying in size and colour from green to yellow to red, ripening in autumn
Cultivation
For fruit or as an ornamental tree, depending on variety
Varieties
USA: *Gravenstein, Jonathan, McIntosh, Yellow Newtown Pippin, Reinette, Golden Delicious, Rome Beauty,* etc. UK: *Bramley's Seedling, Grenadier, Lane's Prince Albert, Russet,* etc.

PEACH *(Prunus persica)*

Family
Rosaceae
Origin
China
Description
Small fruit tree, height up to 30ft (9m)
Leaves
Lance-shaped, sawtoothed; shiny dark green above, paler greyish green beneath
Flowers
Five rounded petals with numerous stamens; varying in colour from pale pink to dark red
Flowering
March or April
Fruit
Nearly round, grooved drupes; sweet, juicy pulp, white or yellow; ripening in summer and very early autumn
Cultivation
For fruit and as an ornamental tree
Varieties
USA: *Elberta, J.H. Hale, Redglobe, Redhaven, Rio Oso Gem, Erligold, Veteran.* UK: *Hale's Early (freestone)*

CURRANT *(Ribes)*

Family
Saxifragaceae (redcurrant, blackcurrant, white currant and gooseberry are members of this category)
Origin
Temperate and warm zones of northern hemisphere, central America and various parts of Andes
Description
Deciduous or evergreen shrub with spines along twigs
Leaves
Ovate or palmate, sawtoothed and distinctly veined; bright green
Flowers
Small and inconspicuous, solitary or in pendulous racemes, they may be yellow, purple, greenish, white tinged with pink, orange or crimson; sometimes fragrant
Flowering
In spring
Fruit
Redcurrants (illustrated) are small, juicy, acidic when ripe; the other varieties in the category can also be black, violet, orange or white, or (gooseberries) green or pale purple
Cultivation
For fruit

PLUM *(Prunus domestica)*

Family
Rosaceae
Origin
Possibly originated in Altai mountains and Turkestan
Description
Small fruit tree growing to approximately 10-22ft / 3-7m and often taller
Leaves
Elliptical or reverse ovate; wavy sawtoothed, pointed at apex; dull green; hairy lower surface
Flowers
Small white, 1-2 flowers on hairy stalks in clusters
Flowering
Early spring
Fruit
Elliptical drupes (round, ovate), bluish-black, violet, purple or yellow; juicy pulp with a pleasant, slightly astringent taste
Cultivation
As a fruit tree
Varieties
USA: *Burbank* (yellowish red skin); *Yellow Egg*; *Greengage* (*Reine Claude*); *Damson, French Damson* (blackish-purple); *Santa Rosa* (crimson purple), *Santa Clara and Shropshire.* UK: *Czar, Pershore Purple, Pershore Yellow Egg, Victoria, Warwickshire Drooper*

GRAPE *(Vitis vinefera)*

Family
Vitaceae
Origin
Southeast Europe to western India
Description
Woody plant, vigorous vines clinging by tendrils to any available support
Leaves
Depending on cultivar, lobed, heartshaped or rounded; glabrous or hairy, light or dark green or reddish-violet
Flowers
Greenish or greenish-yellow in clusters or branches
Flowering
Spring
Fruit
Juicy, fleshy berries, rounded or oval, in bunches or clusters; black, yellow, violet, greenish, etc.
Cultivation
For its fruit
Varieties
Wine varieties are numerous. Table varieties include. *Golden Muscat, Buffalo, Italia, Regina, Olivette Blanche and Ribier*

GLOBE ARTICHOKE *(Cynara cardunculus var. scolymus)*

Family
Compositae
Description
Perennial herbaceous plant, large taproot, strong erect grooved stalk, 16-32in (40-120cm) in height and often higher, dividing into 2 or 3 secondary stems with the flower buds produced terminally, on the stem and on branches originating at the base of the leaves
Leaves
Large, lobed-dentate, spiny, greyish-green above and white and downy beneath, arranged in rosettes at the base or distributed along the stem
Flowers
Heads purple or violet-blue, the receptacle enlarged, fleshy and edible, as are the thickened bases of the unarmed involucral bracts
Fruits
Achenes
Cultivation
Grown for the immature flower receptacles or buds which are cooked and eaten
Varieties
USA: *Green* or *White Globe, Red Dutch, Giant Bud* and *Violet Bud* (probably the same as *Green Globe*). UK & Europe: *Thistle or Prickly Artichoke, Violet Artichoke, French* or *Green French artichoke*

CARROT *(Daucus carota)*

Family
Umbelliferae
Description
Herbaceous plant (annual when cultivated, naturally biennial) with a taproot varying in shape, colour and size. The stalk is erect, grooved, branching and hairy
Leaves
Compound leaves, finely cut into many narrow segments, growing directly from crown on a long stalk; attractive rich deep green
Flowers
Small, white, 5 petals, calyx has 5 sepals; compound flowers in umbels, usually globose
Fruit
Oval, hairy diachenes
Cultivation
Roots grown for human consumption as a vegetable; they can be ground and used as a substitute for coffee
Varieties
USA: *Nantes, Danvers Half Long, Chantenay* (particularly good for canning), *Burpee's Oxheart, Short 'n Sweet, Earliest Short Horn.* UK: *Amsterdam Forcing, Chantenay Redcored*

EGGPLANT / AUBERGINE *(Solanum melongena)*

Family
Solanaceae
Origin
Asia (probably India)
Description
Suffruticose pubescent annual herb or shrub with a rigid, branched stem, erect, reaching heights of 2-3ft (60-90cm) and much more in tropics
Leaves
Large, ovate, angled or slightly lobed, entire or with sinus, covered with fine hair and spines; dull green
Flowers
Solitary, star shaped with violet-purple petals, part sterile, part fertile, with persistent calyx, slightly hairy
Fruits
Large, fleshy, long, oval, round or almost round; skin can vary in colour from purplish-black to violet purple, red or white; off-white, firm flesh, containing numerous small, tender, soft seeds
Cultivation
As a vegetable
Varieties
Black Beauty, Black Magic Hybrid, New Hampshire, Black Pekin (smaller cylindrical fruit); white varieties superior in taste, mainly home grown, rarely available commercially

PEPPER *(Capsicum frutescens,* formerly *capsicum annuum)*

Family
Solanaceae
Origin
South America
Description
Herbaceous annual plant; much branched, erect bushes, more or less glabrous, reaching heights of about 2-3ft (50cm-lm)
Leaves
Ovate or elliptical, simple and entire (smooth-edged), dark green, shiny, varying in size
Flowers
Small, white, borne singly in the axils of the leaves or grouped in threes, corolla wheel shaped
Fruit
A pod-like many-seeded fleshy indehiscent berry varying widely in size, shape, colour and pungency under cultivar
Cultivation
As a vegetable; can be eaten raw or cooked. Some types are dried and ground as seasonings
Varieties
Sweet peppers (var. grossum): *Waltham Beauty, Ruby King, Sweet Yellow.* Cayenne and chilli peppers (var. longum): *Long Red* and *Yellow, Ivory Tusk.* Very hot. Milder peppers: *Grant, Spanish*

TOMATO *(Solanum lycopersicum)*

Family
Solanaceae
Origin
Probably South America
Description
Annual herbaceous plant, with erect stalk, later drooping under weight of fruit, needing support
Leaves
Alternate, pinnately compound, more or less hairy, curled, toothed leaflets; strong odour
Flowers
Nodding, yellow with persistent calyx, produced in clusters or long racemes
Fruit
A pulpy berry, varying in shape and size, smooth, red, watery flesh, containing numerous seeds
Cultivation
As a vegetable (although botanically a fruit)
Varieties
(1) Round, fleshy table tomatoes: *Comet Export, Matchless, Ponderosa.* (2) For preserving or canning (ridged, firm fruit): *Market Wonder, Pierrette, Perfection Indiana Baltimore, Early Baltimore, Greater Baltimore, Ailsa Craig, Moneymaker.* (3) For drying, small fruit in bunches: *King Umberto, Fiaschetta, Small Fry, Gardener's Delight.* (4) For tomato juice: *Rutgers*; for tomato paste (plum type): *St. Marzano*

SQUASH / PUMPKIN *(gen. Cucurbita)*

Family
Cucurbitaceae
Origin
Tropical America
Description
Annual herbaceous plant, bushy or trailing, cylindrical, hollow ridged stems
Leaves
Large, wide, harsh, hairy, palmately lobed
Flowers
Gamopetalous (5 petals), large, funnel-shaped, orange-yellow; borne singly in the axils of the leaves. Either male (staminate) or female (pistillate)
Fruits
These vary tremendously in size, shape and colour. Fleshy pepos. Indehiscent or irregularly bursting
Cultivation
For fruits and flowers, both of which are eaten
Varieties
(1) *Cucurbita maxima* (large fruited, US summer squash, UK marrow). (2) *Cucurbita moschata* or cheese group. (3) *Cucurbita pepo* (common or pumpkin), large and orange, weighing 50lb (22kg) and more. Zucchini/courgette bush has green fruits with light grey, mottled effect. Vegetable marrows can be bush or vine types; US summer squash is a bush type

INDEX

Apple
  and chocolate conserve 29
  and orange jam 24
  (caramelized) jam 31
  chutney 112
  cream 109
  jam, fluffy 29
  sauce 108
Apples
  candied/crystallized 101
  dried 104,191
Apricot
  jam 23
  jelly 55
Apricots
  candied/crystallized 99
  Charterhouse style 79
  dried 104
  in alcohol 80
  in Marsala 79
  in syrup 65
Artichokes
  in brine 125,192-3
  in oil 141
  in spiced vinegar 153
  Italian style 169
Asparagus
  in brine 123
  in vinegar 151
Aubergine, see Eggplant

Banana jam 25
Basil in salt 123
Beans, green/French
  in brine 127
  in tomato sauce 171
  in vinegar 155
Beans, yellow wax/yellow French,
  pickled 155
Beet
  marinated 152
  pickled 151
  preserve 49
Beetroot, see Beet
Bilberry, see Blueberry
Blackberry
  (bramble) jelly 59
  preserve 37
Blackberries in syrup 74
Blackcurrant jelly 60
Blackcurrants in grappa 91
Black Forest jelly 62
Blueberry
  and blackberry jam 40
  preserve 37
Blueberries
  in syrup 73
  with maraschino 89

Cabbage, braised 169
Cape gooseberry jam 35
Capers
  in salt 125
  in vinegar 152
Carrot jam 51
Carrots
  in brine 126
  pickled 153
Cauliflower
  in oil 142, 194
  in vinegar 154
Celery
  in brine 138
  pickled 160
Cherry
  (cornel) jam 39
  (cornel) sauce 107
  jam 27
  jam with honey 16
  (morello) jam 15
  (morello) jelly 55
Cherries
  (cornels) in syrup 67
  in grappa 84
  in spiced vinegar 95
  in syrup 66
  (morello) in alcohol 81
  (morello) in rum 80
  (morello) with purée in rum 81
  sweet-sour 94
Chestnut
  and rum jam 38
  rum balls 84
Citron marmalade 27,187
Corn on the cob, pickled 158
Courgettes, see Zucchini

Damson jam 32

Eggplant preserve 49
Eggplants
  dried 163
  in oil 145
  pickled 158
  sautéed 174
  spiced, salted 131
  with basil 130
  with herbs and tomatoes 174
Elderberry jam 45

Fig and brandy jam 17

Figs
dried, in grappa 85
stuffed, in brandy 85
Fruit
mixed, in aquavit 69
salad 113
salad in syrup 70
salad, in alcohol, mixed berry 87

Garlic in oil 141
Gherkins
in brine 127
in oil 142
pickled 154
Gooseberry jelly 61
Grape
jelly 21
preserve, old-fashioned 21
Grapes
in grappa 93, 190
in liqueur 94
in syrup 76
Grapefruit
in syrup 75
jelly 59

Jujube jelly 39
Jujubes in alcohol 87

Leeks
curried 180
in brine 137
Lemon
and apple conserve 17
curd 111
flip 111
Lettuce, marinated 159

Mandarin jelly 57
Mandarins in syrup 70
Mango jam 28
Marrons glacés 100
Melon jam 19
Melons
in syrup 73
in their own syrup 71
Mint and apple jam 46
Mushrooms
alla cacciatora 171
dried 163
in oil 144
in oil with basil 144
in salt 129
in spiced brine 129, 130
in vinegar 157, 195
marinated 157
Piedmont style 173
piquant, in oil 143

Olive
and anchovy compote 175
spread 175
Olives
in brine 131
in oil, Andalusian style 145
in tuna, tomato and herb sauce 176
Onions
pickled 155
pickled, in oil 143
piquant 170
sweet-sour 170, 196
Orange
and lemon marmalade 24, 186
crunch 113
flower and apple preserve 43
jelly 56
peel, candied/crystallized 99
sauce 107
Oranges
in alcohol 82, 189
in grappa 83
in syrup 66

Parsley
dried 165
in oil 147
Peach jam 32
Peaches
candied/crystallized 102
in liqueur 91
in spiced mild vinegar 96
in syrup 74
Pear
jam 31
preserve 19
preserve, spiced 20
Pears
candied/crystallized 102
in grappa 89
marinated 95
Peas
Gourmet's 179
in brine 133
Peperonata 177
Persimmon
jam 25
jelly 56
Pineapple
and kiwi fruit jam 23
conserve, sweet-sour 16
in kirsch 82
jam 15
rings in syrup 65

Plum
jelly 61
preserve 20
Plums
in aquavit 93
in syrup 75
sweet-sour 96
Prickly pear jam 46
Pumpkin
candied/crystallized 103
jam 51

Quince
and sugar-beet jam 28
cheese 112

Radicchio rosso, see Treviso radish
Raspberry
jelly 57
preserve 36
Raspberries in syrup 69
Red summertime preserve 38
Redcurrant sauce, sweet-sour 108
Rhubarb
in syrup 76
jam 50
Rose petal
and apple preserve 43
and fruit jam 45

Salsify, see Scorzonera
Sauerkraut 126
Scorzonera
in brine 137
Piedmont style 181
Sorb apple
jam 40
jelly 60
Spinach, Piedmont style 183
Strawberry
preserve 36
sauce 109
Strawberries in syrup 67
Sweet chestnut and brandy preserve 35
Sweet chestnuts
in kirsch 83
in syrup 71
Sweet (bell) pepper jam 50
Sweet (bell) peppers
in brine 133
in oil 147
pickled 159
Puglia style 176, 197
stuffed 177

Tomato
(green) jam 52, 188
jam 52
juice 135
paste/purée with vegetables 179
paste/purée 135
sauce 134
Tomatoes
dried 164
dried, with basil 164
preserved whole 134
Treviso radish in oil 148
Truffles in wine 181

Vegetable
brochettes, pickled 180
Caprice 183
medley, sweet-sour 173
relish, sweet-sour 184
Vegetables, salted mixed soup 138
Vinegar
flavoured with four herbs 165
raspberry-flavoured red wine 166
rose petal 166
tarragon 166
Violets, candied/crystallized 103

Wine jelly 62

Zucchini
in oil 148
marinated, Puglia style 160
marinated, Rumanian style 184